A Case for Peace
in Reason and Faith

Monika K. Hellwig

A Michael Glazier Book
THE LITURGICAL PRESS
Collegeville, Minnesota

A Michael Glazier Book published by The Liturgical Press

Cover design by Fred Petters

1   2   3   4   5   6   7   8   9

Library of Congress Cataloging-in-Publication Data

Hellwig, Monika.
   A case for peace in reason and faith / Monika K. Hellwig.
      p.   cm.
   "A Michael Glazier book."
   Includes bibliographical references.
   ISBN 0-8146-5834-2
   1. Peace—Religious aspects. 2. War—Religious aspects. 3. Peace.
4. War. I. Title.
BL65.P4H45   1992
291.1'7873—dc20

                                                                92-13670
                                                                CIP

To Michael and Joan Glazier,
whose inspired work in religious publishing
evoked great outpourings of creativity and scholarship
from authors known and unknown
and left the religious literature of our times
greatly enriched.

Contents

Acknowledgments

My gratitude is due especially to the editors of The Liturgical Press; to Rev. Kevin Lynch, C.S.P., who gave the project his kindly encouragement from the beginning; to John Dear and other friends of Pax Christi whose unflagging devotion to the cause of peace have drawn attention to the many facets of work for peace; to Mr. Carl Landegger whose generosity in funding the Landegger Professorship with a summer research grant enabled me to spend the time needed for this book; to Rev. Richard McSorley, S.J., a prophet for peace in season and out of season on the Georgetown University campus and across the world; to the conscientious objectors of the Vietnam and Gulf Wars who carried the burden for all of us; to Rev. Eugene Rooney, S.J., librarian of the Woodstock library for help far beyond the call of duty; to my colleagues in the Georgetown University Theology Department for their friendly encouragement of my writing; and to the many authors cited in the notes and bibliography who had already done the detailed research that made a broader synthesis possible.

Introduction: An Issue We Must Face

Death by violence has always been tragic, and war has always meant killing, maiming, blinding, hurting people, destroying livelihoods and property, instilling fear, hatred, and revenge. War creates new suffering on a massive scale and initiates new injustices. Moreover, the burden has always fallen disproportionately on the poor and powerless, who do not have the resources to protect or insulate themselves from the death and suffering caused by massive armed conflict sweeping through their homelands.

These are facts that people have always known, and yet there have been wars. Parents have wept for their innocent sons, killed as pawns in the game, wives for their husbands, children for their fathers. Now we are in a new phase, and we have learned to weep for our daughters blown apart, for wives gunned down, for mothers who do not return. Yet all along, in the lands of the conquered and in the homes of their poor and defenseless, old and young, sick and well, male and female, have died as the price paid for someone else's sense of right and wrong, of proper law and order, of national vindication, if not actually of national aggrandizement. But history is written more usually by the victorious, not by the conquered, by the rulers and decision makers, and not by the poor and powerless or the foot soldiers who bear the brunt of the battle. History is not written about the pain and agony of the wounded and the dying or about the heartache of those who mourn and those who are crippled, blinded, or made limbless for life, but rather about

9

the victory celebrations, the magnificent speeches, the new arrangements of power.

No sane person wishes evil for its own sake. Governments who declare war usually do so with reluctance, explaining to their constituencies that war has become necessary for moral reasons or inevitable for strategic reasons. In fact, as weaponry has become more and more powerful and sophisticated, making more and more damage possible in a single attack, the reluctance has become more explicit. Popular protests against war have become more numerous and persistent, and internal struggles within governments debating war or preparing for it have become more publicly evident. No one really wants war. Therefore, it is important to keep raising the question of the reasons given for war, why it is seen as resolving existing conflicts and injustices, why it is seen as the only workable solution, even a necessary or inevitable solution.

For thousands of years human beings have worked out ways of arbitration and negotiation to deal with conflicts. In our time, at the national level and among certain clusters of allied nations, there is a firm commitment to resolve conflicts in these ways. A body of laws has been developed to make that possible, and machinery has been put in place to ensure smooth and continuous administration of the laws applicable to various types of conflicting interests. Yet in spite of much progress in diplomatic conflict resolution in the medieval period, and in spite of the modern formation of the League of Nations, and its reconstitution as the United Nations, we continue to have frequent recourse to wars among the nations of the world as the chosen means of attempting to resolve major injustices. It is not the means that are lacking for non-violent conflict resolution, nor is it a theory or legal tradition. There is a network of resistance more entrenched than that, more pervasive in human consciousness, more elusive to critical examination.

The purpose of this book is to invite reflection, first by the light of reason and then by the light of religious faith, on the logic that promotes war and the logic that promotes peace. We, the human race, will never come to the end of wars unless many people begin at the grass-roots level to become critically aware of the practical values operative in their lives and the way those practical values compare with the expressed values of their religious and cultural traditions. As the world becomes smaller through technology and communications, and as the power of destruction becomes larger, the need for such reflection and for self-critical awareness becomes more and more urgent. At the same time, as the world becomes smaller through convergence of experiences and language, through the sharing of scientific knowledge and technical power, and through more widespread access to literacy and to education of all kinds, there is also increased opportunity for more critical awareness of our own operational values and expectations.

This is a time of opportunity for peace in a larger and more thorough sense than ever before, but it is an opportunity that must be seized by the truly human activity of critical reflection.

1

War Is Not the Answer: The Logic of Reason

We tell our children not to fight, but to talk it out until they find a solution to any conflict that arises, and if necessary to appeal to arbitration by third parties. We urge individual citizens not to take matters into their own hands by violence and revenge, but to seek police protection when necessary, and to obtain redress through the courts. We expect groups of disadvantaged and oppressed people in democracies to turn to lobbying, demonstrations, airing of grievances through the press, and so forth, rather than starting riots, assassinating people, or destroying property. We do all this by the logic of reason: physical might is not necessarily right. Being stronger or more violent does not equate with having a more just cause. Sheer common sense can assure us of that much by way of negation, and something more by way of affirmation.

Positively, we assume that human beings are capable of resolving human problems humanely, that is to say through intelligent reflection. One of the basic principles of such intelligent reflection as a means of problem solving is the proposition that we are relational and communitarian beings interdependent for existence and for everything that makes existence worthwhile. This interdependence will function smoothly and supportively if all of us treat others as we ourselves would want to be treated in their situation. Our own experiences and the bridges into the experience of others which our capacity for empathy makes available do in fact equip us to understand how we would want to be treated if we were in the situation of the others. Yet it is perhaps at this point of the need and opportunity for correct empathizing that human relations most frequently begin to break down.

Short-sighted Self-interest

The logic of reason is clear, but the logic of a short-sighted self-interest often intervenes. The short-sighted message in its crudest form runs like this: I have the power to compel (or we as a group have the power to maintain the present state of affairs), so it is irrelevant to consider what the subordinate party experiences, or would like to experience; indeed the subordinate party should be grateful that we are maintaining this state of affairs and not something worse. This short-sighted self-interest is usually legitimated by justifying arguments that sound correct within the cultural expectations of the particular society. Some of these are as follows. We must maintain a dictatorial regime because the poor and uneducated are always so prone to violence. Or, we must unfortunately dominate in this harsh way because the people have not yet developed the mentality and motivations of the truly socialist or communist society. Or again, it is really necessary to maintain this order under which many remain poor and excluded in order to boost the economy, because eventually the benefits will trickle down to all, though never equally to all. Or once more, the human community faces stiff competition for scarce resources, and there will inevitably always be some very wealthy at one extreme and others destitute at the other, so that the most that can be done is to look out for oneself and one's interest group and defend the wealthy against the destitute so that there will not be total scarcity or total chaos.

The reason for designating all these arguments and positions "short-sighted self-interest" is twofold: on the one hand, they cannot work even for the privileged in the long run; and there exists, on the other hand, according to the strict logic of reason in human affairs, a truly enlightened long-term self-interest which can work. The reason these arguments and positions are short-sighted and unenlightened lies in our interdependence, in our dependence on natural resources, and in biological factors. The slave-owner, the employer, the big spender and conspicuous consumer, are all in fact more dependent on their counterparts than vice versa. Poverty, deprivation, margination from the services of technological society, begin by affecting the underprivileged but end by spreading disease and contamination, by weakening the producers of wealth and therefore reducing the available wealth, and by many other conditions which cannot be neatly contained among the ranks of the underprivileged. At the same time there is an enlightened and long-term self-interest which is rooted in our interdependence, and which must be explored further in this volume.

The application of short-sighted self-interest such as has just been described is often alleged as the reason for violent solutions at individual, small-group, local, regional, and national levels. It is, for instance, invoked for the imprisonment, execution, and harsh treatment of young men of underclass racial or economic groups in several countries in our time. Recent history has made it abundantly clear that while such repression may briefly hold back the tide of chaos and civil war, it does not create a lasting peace within the society because the real cause of unrest, namely, the oppression and lack of opportunity for full participation in society, has not been addressed by a policy of repression of actual, potential, or perceived violence of the underclass by greater violence on the part of those in privilege and power. Similarly, such reasons of self-defense on the part of the society (that is, of its dominant groups) have frequently been alleged in modern history in cases of explicitly declared or practically effective genocide or large-scale expulsion of ethnic groups. Again, history has proved that such moves of violence do not protect those who make them but initiate a further complex dynamic of destructive hostilities.

War, No Answer to Conflicts

War is not the answer to conflicts among nations for a number of reasons evident to common sense. The most evident of these is that armed violence on any scale is not capable of determining or demonstrating who is right. By its very nature physical violence determines who is stronger or who is more ruthless. In battles between nations, armed violence usually results in the victory of the

side that is more numerous, and in battles depending on high technology, it favors even more the side that has the more sophisticated
weapons or has them in greater abundance. That has been the history of colonialism. In many cases we can look back and see conquest of other lands out of sheer greed, followed by the subjugation
and sometimes the extermination of the indigenous inhabitants.
History books have glorified these conquests as courageous adven-
tures of loyal and patriotic service to one's own nation. But that
is because the history books have been written from the perspective of the conquerors, not from the perspective of the conquered
or the slain.

   If we look at the wars of colonial expansion with the eyes of
common sense and common decency, we can see very easily that
those who won were those who were in the wrong because they
were unjust aggressors. Military conflict did not vindicate the rights
of the conquered to their own lands; it assured victory to those
who had more destructive weapons, better transportation, and
often greater numbers. Similarly, when we look at the conflicts in
modern times, detached observers have voiced serious questions
whether those who won the armed conflict were morally better
or worse in their cause and in their conduct of the war than those
who lost.

War, the Cause of Injustice

   While this lack of intrinsic correspondence of might with right
is clearly the most compelling argument of common sense against
war, it is by no means the only one. A second important argument
is that in those many wars which have avowedly been fought to
right an injustice, many other injustices have been caused by the
wars themselves—the killing, maiming, blinding, disfiguring, and
psychological destruction of both soldiers and civilians; the destruction of people's homes and fields, of things that are precious to
them and things that are beautiful; the creation of terror, despair,
revenge, and hatred, which do not end when the victory is declared.
Conventional wisdom about the ethics of war has focused on the
treatment of civilians and has seen the killing of civilians as an af-
front to human decency. It is good, of course, that such an attitude has been expressed, but it has bypassed the question of the

killing of soldiers in horrible ways and in terrible agony. Soldiers in major wars in modern times have been conscripts; their vote was not asked on whether the war would be declared or whether they were willing to fight in it. They have always been predominantly young, and often predominantly the less privileged and less educated, at least in the front lines or positions of greatest vulnerability. Whatever injustice may or may not be put right by an armed conflict, it is paid for by the injustice visited upon those who die and suffer, predominantly the young and the poor. It is a question we cannot afford to neglect, in what way the sacrificing of these people against their will, without their choice, is to be celebrated as a great triumph of freedom and justice.

Least at Stake, First Sacrificed in War

To this second reason may be added a third. Those who are sacrificed in war are in almost all cases those who have least at stake in the settlement of the issues over which the war is fought. This case has been made, for instance, for Afro-American soldiers in recent wars involving the United States, but it has always been the case for peasants and the urban poor. The struggles for power, for national independence or foreign trade opportunities, have offered them no advantages in return for loss of life and limb and mental health. Those who declare wars are in the nature of the case people of power and influence. Their position in society keeps them well away from the actual horrors of battle, from the terror and the weariness, and the agonizing pain of wounds, not to mention the lifelong aftermath of nightmares, guilt, disablement, and other terrible consequences shaping all future experience for those who have been in the heat of the action. Moreover, those who decide to make war are not the military who are burdened with the crushing responsibility of actual use of kill-power. The decision to make war takes place in remote and insulated comfort in which the decision makers can deal with human pain and misery by reducing it to statistical abstractions. It is from such safe isolation that the decision makers weigh the cost in human life and pain which they consider worth paying for a strategic advantage of some sort in the international balancing of power. It is a fact of everyday experience that the pain and misery of others, especially those who are distant from us or not personally known, tends to weigh very lightly in the balance against anything that we ourselves want.

Need for Negotiation

Even more important, and evident to commonsense reflection on past wars, is the fact that the real issues over which the wars have been fought usually have to be settled by negotiation after the wars have officially ended. But this raises the question why the negotiations are not begun without fighting the war. Often the grievances of the conquered party are not dealt with and simmer until they break out eventually into another war. A case in point is World War I, settled so arrogantly by the winning powers that the result exploded with much increased violence in World War II, after which the real problems of the conquered were finally given some attention. These two wars did incalculable harm, inflicting unimaginable suffering and a staggering number of deaths. They did not offer a brave new world, a newfound freedom, or a better share in the earth's resources to the hordes of people who died in terror and pain. For them there was nothing gained but much lost by the wars. Those who survived gained, if at all, not by the wars but by the negotiations that followed, and this raises the inexorable question whether the wars were really the only way of proceeding to the negotiations or whether they may actually have been a hindrance to future relations between countries.

Realizing the Objectives of War in Other Ways

While these four arguments suggest that war is not the answer because it does not lead to the greater common good and does not even guarantee the victory to the party with the better moral claim to be in the right, there are also arguments that war is not the answer because the stated objectives can be realized in more effective ways. Perhaps the most important of those positive arguments lies in the true nature of national security. In recent decades this term "national security" has been invoked a great deal, especially in the United States, as an argument for building a larger arsenal of weapons, for demonstrating readiness to use them, and for initiating acts of war whenever there appears to be a threat to the existing structure of dominance in economic and political relations. But this rests on a false understanding of what constitutes security. An individual, group, or nation is most secure when no one has a reason to attack that party. And no one has a reason to attack when relationships are mutually helpful and friendly, that is when each has something to gain from the others by exchange of goods and services. The poorer and weaker nations of the world, like poor and weak groups and individuals, have always been keenly aware of this. The temptation to seek national security by building greater power to destroy is a temptation that besets powerful and rich nations. But it rests on a failure of empathy and of common sense.

The understanding that the nation's security depends on exceeding others in kill-power leaves much out of the reckoning. In the first place, it already assumes a state of open or covert hostility as the posture of the others, and the more the strategy of greater kill-power is pursued, the more likely it is that hostile intentions will be projected onto the others which were not already there. If, however, the conjecture is correct that there are hostile intentions, then this shows that the hostile others are either smarting under a grievance or afraid of attack from the first (our) side. If they see us as a continuing threat with our arms buildup, they are driven to compete by increasing their own kill-power. The long "cold war" between the Soviet sector and the industrial West demonstrated this to the point of absurdity, and at the end of it the real threat to national security has been revealed as the internal disintegration of the Soviet Union from local grievances long unattended, and internal upheaval in the United States from physical and social deterioration of the cities, a faltering economy with an endangered banking system, inability to give medical care to all who need it while there is a rampant AIDS epidemic, and increasing debility from drug and alcohol abuse. The real national security needs and foundations were obscured by spiraling reciprocal projection of hostile intention onto the other side by each of the giant partners in the "cold war."

Moreover, the whole history of the world shows that there is a dangerous psychological error in the supposition that people will settle down to subordinate, marginated, or deprived status simply by being bullied and threatened enough. The history of the world suggests the reverse; bitter grievances keep smoldering and intensifying until the pressure becomes intolerable and the whole situation erupts like a volcano. It happened in Roman times with groups like the *sicarii* and the Zealots, it happened throughout history with slave and peasant revolts, and in our own times it spawns guerilla movements and worldwide terrorist networks.

Careful reflection on twentieth-century developments in the Middle East should make it clear to any observer that national security is increased when there are mutually satisfactory agreements with neighboring peoples and internal minorities, and that national security becomes impossible when grievances of neighboring peoples and internal minorities are allowed to accumulate and continue unresolved. There is no national security where street violence, riots, and terrorist attacks are liable to break out anywhere at any time. No matter how strong the military power of the dominant group, everyone lives in fear to greater or lesser degree all the time in such a situation.

Along with this argument from the nature of national security, goes an argument from the nature of the human person, which everyone can understand from personal experience. Individuals feel at peace and at ease when they are able to feel that they are in control of their own lives. They feel energized and motivated when they are able to plan and to execute their plans, to take initiatives in relationships and to experience reciprocity in their relationships, to work for the common good because they know that their own individual well-being is an integral part of the common good, to be concerned for others because their own basic needs are being met. Most of us can think of situations in which we have been at ease and in which we felt empowered to do worthwhile things, but we can also think of situations in which because of ethnic, sexual, regional, somatic type, cultural, or other prejudices, we felt disabled, disregarded, marginated, and therefore profoundly dissatisfied with our role in the situation and with our relationships with others. There is a restlessness in such situations which sooner or later becomes an open conflict.

People of a dominant or aggressive personality type may think that the best way to get things done is dictatorially, by "showing who's boss," but the true wisdom of "management techniques" is that contented workers who feel that they are an integral part of the shaping of the enterprise will work most productively and smoothly together. This is true of relationships and working partnerships of individuals, and it is true of groups and teams of all sizes. It is equally true of nations and of ethnic or regional groups within nations. That, of course, is the underlying principle of democracy; participation in decision making and the shaping of the society not only guarantees the share of each group in the goods of the society but corresponds to the true human nature of all the people involved. To enjoy the fulness of one's human nature means, among other aspects, to be creative and self-determining as far as that is possible in community with others.

Problem Solving According to Reason

This project of creativity and self-determination within community with others is possible, according to reason, based on two human faculties which can be cultivated to a greater or lesser extent: empathy and enlightened self-interest. It is possible to know the experience of others by analogies with our own experience. It is possible to build a bridge into the thoughts, feelings, affections, and loyalties of others by our human capacity for empathy, to put oneself into the position of others in order to understand the logic of their loyalties, actions, and expectations. This human capacity for empathy, fully exercised, does not suggest war or efforts to dominate as a solution to problems or conflicts among peoples. It suggests rather some study and reflection to try to understand how we ourselves would like to be approached if we were in the position of the others, and what terms or conditions would make a positive and constructive response most likely.

The other dimension of problem solving according to reason is enlightened self-interest. Countries declare war expecting to be better off after winning a war. Enlightened self-interest, however, should focus on two facts of warfare: first, that the outcome is seldom assured, and second, that war involves death, injuries, and destruction of valuable resources for both sides. If it is possible to attain the same objectives without the destruction, the reasonable choice is to follow the alternative to war. But this can be assumed to be possible because it is in the enlightened self-interest of both parties to the dispute. Both will be materially better off, and will suffer less if the matter is resolved by negotiation. Moreover, in the modern world we have many structures in place which can regulate negotiations between nations with a certain neutrality.

It is clear that while the advantages of negotiation to both sides are evident in the abstract, they are seldom recognized in concrete cases. In practice wars are started from motives of greed, fear, and desperation. They arise from greed when wealthy and powerful countries want to expand their economies further beyond their boundaries and meet resistance. They arise from fear when governments see threats of attack that may not even be there in reality, and when they therefore resort to preemptive strikes. And wars arise from desperation when those who suffer injustices, oppression, and destitution can find no other way to make their voices heard in the public arena. These last are usually guerilla-type campaigns or terrorist activities. In many concrete cases reason does not prevail because greed, fear, and desperation are stronger. That is why faith is indispensable in human affairs. Faith must offer a vision of true and possible harmony in human community, as well as an explanation of what has gone wrong to cause such massive, self-destructive violence in human history, and a path of reconciliation which can overcome violence and attain to the harmony which is the proper condition of human life. Almost all faiths offer some such vision, explanation, and path, and closer attention shows enough convergence to make extensive cooperation possible in the quest for peace in the world.

2

No More War: A Hope Informed by Faith

Most people, reading chapter 1 of this book, would say that the arguments are all very well in the abstract world of the philosopher or the mathematician, but that the real world is full of intractable problems that are not soluble by reason and in which people therefore resort to force. We have all had the experience in dealing with people that what is reasonable is not what always happens. Prejudice, selfishness, greed for more wealth, lust for more power, the pursuit of one's own pleasure at any cost to others, unwillingness to get involved in matters that offer no personal profit, suspicion, fear, revenge, and many other forces defying reason enter into the picture.

Limits of Reason in Human Affairs

There are basically three ways in which human philosophies and religions respond to this realization about the limits of reason in human affairs. One response is to say that evil, suffering, and chaotic destruction are inevitable in the world in which we find ourselves, and the best that anyone can do is to create a little order and predictable social patterns around oneself and one's family, group, class, or nation, to the extent that it proves possible, for as long as possible, while not expecting too much. A second response is to say that in the material, social, historical realm of human experience, there is no solution to the plurality of self-determining beings with their competing spontaneities in a fragile material context, so that the only solution is to look for spiritual peace within oneself. A third response is to assert a transcendent resource out of which we can draw a strength greater than reason to overcome human conflict. There is, of course, a rather small number of people who commit themselves to a fourth option because they do not accept the premise about the inadequacy of human reason to resolve conflict; they do expect reason to prevail and to end wars along with other expressions of violence as the solution to human conflict.[1]

The first response just described is a cynical one. It does not allow for a community embracing all human beings. It does not expect much for any human being or for any human community because it amounts to an endorsement of the principle of the survival of the strongest accompanied by the discarding of the others as wastage. Indirectly such a response endorses and justifies violence as the way human affairs must inevitably be run. The reason implicit in this position for the justification of violence or brute force as the governing principle in human affairs is an implicit or explicit belief that in the final analysis reality is chaotic, having no overarching design, purpose, or cohesion. Unfortunately, this type of response to problems of human conflict is frequently designated "realist," even by those who do not agree with it, as though other responses were less in touch with reality than this one. Yet all the responses listed are dealing with what is actually happening, but the difference between them consists of the way they interpret that same reality and its possibilities for change or transformation.

The second response, the one that looks for peace only within oneself, but not in the world, is a common one, but it is a counsel of despair because it implies an abdication of all responsibility for what is going on in the world. This is contrary to all the biblical religions, Judaism, Christianity, and Islam, and comes directly or indirectly into conflict with the tenets of the other great religions. It is contrary to the biblical religions because the doctrine of creation asserts a single source and sustainer of all that is, a source which is benign and powerful, creating order out of chaos and bringing all things into harmony with human cooperation. The biblical religions invoke a set of divine commandments for the conduct of human affairs, so that the divine purpose may be fully realized and all creatures may profit from the harmony intended in creation. Such an interpretation of reality does not allow the followers of these religions to excuse themselves from social and worldly responsibilities on the pretext of cultivating an inner peace for their private benefit alone. But even apart from the specific doctrine of creation in the biblical traditions, all the great traditions of the world, as well as the local religious traditions which have been studied and recorded, have elaborated rules for human conduct which are calculated to achieve harmony in society and thus bring peace.

Besides being incompatible with the religious traditions, the second response, looking only for an inward peace and not for peace in the world, does not reflect the truth about human existence. Human beings are both spiritually and materially interdependent with one another. This interdependence is constitutive of our very existence; we are not spirits or minds accidentally incorporated in material organisms; we are living bodies, each born of another, each fed, clothed, and housed by the cooperation of many others working in many different ways. In our days especially, of course, that network of interdependence is no longer merely local, regional, or national, but worldwide and very complex. There is, in fact, no lasting peace for any of us, in the full sense of peace, while any part of the human race in any part of the world is being ignored or excluded, and there certainly is no true peace at the cost of denying social and worldly responsibilities. The reason for introducing the word "worldly" in addition to the word "social" is that as corporeal beings we are intimately interdependent not only with one another but also with the physical universe in which we live and with all other living beings in that same universe. It is an integral part of the realization of the truth of our being to be aware of the physical universe and the ecological interdependence of the living beings and the inanimate resources. Moreover, it is an integral part of acting according to the truth of our being to accept the responsibility for stewardship which is implicit in human intelligence and the human capacity for creativity, adaptation, invention, planning.

Because the rest of this chapter will be devoted to the third response, it may be worthwhile here to say something briefly about the fourth response. It is true that theoretically reason should be able to resolve all problems of human conflicts of interest. Yet observation shows that this is not happening because reasonable arguments do not always have the motivational and emotional power to ensure appropriate action. We come face to face with the fact that people often let disordered desires take over, and that over long periods of time and large numbers of interacting groups this leaves a situation in which doing the reasonable thing is simply not enough. There is often such a tangled web of the consequences of past selfish and greedy choices that it is possible to agree in theory that war and violence are not the answer and yet find in practice that reasonable solutions are very difficult to find and very slow to take effect. Most people, therefore, are not sure enough from their own experience that reason will work because the answers called for are not only reasonable but heroic, requiring reconciliation in relationships already fraught with anger, fear, and grief. Under such circumstances people need hope that evil can be overcome, and therefore they need solid grounds for such hope. Most people of the earth find the grounds for their hope in a religious faith tradition which has taught them to look for power and wisdom which comes from beyond themselves, infusing new possibilities into apparently insoluble problems.

The Response of Religious Faith

That is the logic and persuasive force behind the third response. This response which looks to a transcendent resource begins with a sober assessment that ordinary human resources are inadequate to the challenge of peace and harmony in human society. So at the outset this response is in agreement with the first response. But where the first response accepts this inadequacy as a closed situation, the third response, which is typically that of religious faith, looks for further options and finds them in a transcendent source for human empowerment. That empowerment works through conversion from destruction to life, alternately presented in some traditions as primarily a conversion to a way of wisdom.

There is, however, a difficulty in presenting and in accepting this position. It is possible to look through the literature and the actual history of Judaism, Christianity, and Islam, and at various times incidents or phases in the other religious traditions, and find there some very warlike expressions in word and deed. We can even find the divine represented as a Warrior God leading an army of human subjects into battle against other peoples in a holy cause. There is no doubt that this constitutes a considerable embarrassment for those who look to their religious traditions for the wisdom and power that makes peace. Some Christian scholars have resolved the difficulty by acknowledging the concept of Holy War or Crusade and the concept of Justified War for defense as part of the revelation in a world so distorted by sin that a kind of surgical intervention is needed. Others have pointed out an admixture of human ignorance and confusion in the religious tradition, even in formulations of the Sacred Scriptures. We can in fact trace a development from a more primitive understanding of God as a tribal God of one people to the understanding of God as the great creator of all, God of all peoples, desiring peace and harmony among all. Some Islamic scholars have looked at the idea of Holy War simply as prerequisite to bringing all peoples into submission to Allah and to the divine law that should govern societies as well as individuals. Other voices in Islam, for instance among the Sufi, have been more radically critical of wars of conquest. Similarly in Jewish tradition voices justifying wars have done this with the vision of a greater peace when Yahweh's rule is extended to the furthest islands, while other voices have simply preached peace.[2] Commentators on classic Hindu literature have sometimes presented warring gods as personifications of the forces we know in our human lives and in the world about us.[3]

What can be gathered from looking at the major traditions is that none praise war and conquest for their own sake. At most the commentators and spokespersons try to justify what they admit looks utterly unjustifiable in the light of the basic teachings of each tradition. It is clear that those who speak for the traditions, whether by virtue of office or by virtue of scholarship, feel hard pressed to find an explanation that would in any measure justify or excuse endorsement of violence and war, while a return to the sources of the traditions and critical analysis of the developments within the traditions reveal a radical quest for peace in each of them. Meanwhile, one of the greatest, oldest, and most widespread religious traditions of the world, Buddhism, has carried a strong, continuous, and unquestioned message of peace and non-violence as both possible and necessary.[4]

The Response of Non-Christian Traditions

While Christianity in its various strains continues to be the dominant religion of the western world and its outposts, it is important to note that the foundations for a theory and practice of peace which are found in the Judaeo-Christian heritage also find echoes and counterparts in the other traditions which are strong in our world. Moreover, the explicit separation of Church and state in the United States and the implicit banishment of religious considerations from public policy prevailing in other western countries is not found in the same degree elsewhere. Because the other traditions have not gone through the western experience of the Enlightenment, the reciprocal penetration of religion and culture (including political life and organization) is much more pervasive and much less critically questioned. The resources in the religious traditions of these other peoples of the world are even more politically relevant to the pursuit of peace than they are for the historically Christian peoples of the increasingly secularized West.

Because traditional religions play this large role in many societies, and because the peace of each nation is today inseparable from the peace of all other nations, it is important to realize that the fundamental precept forbidding killing is not unique to the commandments of the Mosaic Law and the traditions which acknowledge that Law. In ancient Hindu mythology, in which gods seem to wage reckless war, apparently describing forces at work in the world rather than prescribing for human conduct, there is a gradual emergence of critical reflection on the effects of violence. Most movingly, in the Bhagavad Gita, Arjuna the warrior is appalled over the destruction that war would bring, and turns away. Brahmin tradition favored figurative interpretation of the ancient texts with their warring gods. Attention was focused on the doctrine of the Upanishads about the oneness of the human spirit with world soul and the consequent oneness of each with other living beings. Not surprisingly, therefore, a way of salvation by meditation and realization becomes also a way of *ahimsa* or non-injury to others.[5]

In the teaching of Siddhartha Gautama, the Buddha, and of Mahavira, the founder of the Jains, *ahimsa* became a central and critical requirement for true followers, and seekers after the saving truth. The great conquering Emperor Asoka, having become a Buddhist, ended his wars of expansion and tried to create a realm of peace, even becoming a vegetarian. Though the Parsis have never been numerous in India, the Zoroastrian teachings which they introduced when they fled there, converged with this trend of thought. They also envisaged a great cosmic battle, but it was entirely in the moral realm, a struggle between those good, constructive, and uplifting patterns of behavior which make for harmony and well-being on the one hand and those untruthful, dishonest, destructive patterns of behavior which make for chaos and suffering.

In the practical world of politics this history became very important for the twentieth century. Mohandas Gandhi was able to draw on those strands of the Indian traditions which honored and promoted a non-violent way of life and of conflict resolution in order to mount a movement for independence of the subcontinent, so disciplined and so restrained that a major war with massive bloodshed was avoided while the goal of independence was met. The fact that conflicts between Muslims and Hindus subsequently exploded into occasional violence, and that tensions between Sikhs and Hindus remain a threat, does nothing to diminish the moral and practical exemplary force of Gandhi's *swaraj* movement for the whole world. Significant in that example is the fact that Gandhi himself acknowledged that he found the inspiration and support for non-violent action both in the traditions of India and in the religious heritage of the British against whom he was asserting Indian independence. It was a stance which he thought the British could be made to understand because the Gospel of Jesus Christ contained a central *ahimsa* doctrine too.[6]

The Message of Non-violence

As is well known, the vision and the success of the Mahatma sparked a new interest in the gospel teaching of non-violence which is usually translated "meekness." Martin Luther King and the United States civil rights movement employed the same principle of non-violent protest to obtain radical legislative and social restructuring of race relations. King and his close collaborators were able to invoke traditional biblical themes of the Christian faith to claim nationwide loyalty and solidarity not only for the cause but for a non-violent way of conducting the campaign. Since then, non-violence has become a well-established idea and much thought has been given to its development as an ascetic tradition. In the non-violent revolution against the Marcos dictatorship in the Philippines, the discipline of *ahimsa* had been so well assimilated and perfected that it succeeded without the brutalities called forth from the dominant side by Gandhi's pioneering movement or by Martin Luther King's campaign. That may have been due to many factors, but one of them was certainly that the political power of non-violence had been illustrated in these earlier cases, and the project of a non-violent revolution no longer looked like something that could be lightly discounted. Moreover, the peaceful revolution in the Philippines not only had the support of the institutional Catholic Church, but was mainly brought about by the leadership of church professionals in collaboration with deeply committed lay leaders who acted from religious convictions.

Spirituality: Incompatible with Aggression

What has come about in the twentieth century, especially within the Christian tradition, is that the long-accepted understanding that spirituality is incompatible with aggression and violence, has been discovered as an active force, not only a passive condition. The New Testament, in proposing meekness, non-vengeance, non-cupidity, abstention from status and power seeking, did in fact release a revolutionary force in society. Yet for many centuries the social, economic, and political transformations that came about were not the outcome of explicit goal setting, planning, and strategy for the shape of society. They came about almost imperceptibly. Consequently they were seen as the work of God operating in mysterious ways, in response to prayer, or as a reward for devout and law-abiding lives. In other words, except in times of active persecution when civil disobedience was clearly the duty of believers, it seemed that the continuing work of divine providence in the world required the faithful to be passive in their acceptance of social, political, and economic power as exercised in their societies.

From time to time that passive acceptance of civil authorities also involved fighting, killing, and destroying when those authorities declared war.

What has emerged from the cross-fertilization of traditions, beginning with the active *ahimsa* of the *swaraj* movement in India, is the awakening sense in traditionally Christian countries, that the transforming power of the Christian gospel is one that calls not for a static social inactivity but for a non-violent style of radical social critique and collaborative action. Long ago, at the beginning of the third century of the common era in Alexandria in Egypt, the Christian writer Origen stated that while the wars of the empire might be unavoidable, Christians should not fight in them because they had a better way of dealing with barbarian invasions of their homes. His better way was martyrdom, the witness to the truth by death. After his time this became more problematic because the empire gradually became Christian, and Christians carried its civic responsibilities. Therefore in the early fifth century of the common era, Augustine of Hippo felt obliged to write with great reluctance that under certain conditions of desperation, even Christians must be allowed to defend their homes and families against invaders. This opinion of Augustine depended heavily on the sad conclusion that there was no other way, there being no possibility of diplomatic negotiations with the barbarians.

Whatever the possibilities of the actual situation in his time, the authority of Augustine as an interpreter of Christian faith and life does not support warfare in conditions in which any possibility of negotiation remains. In fact, in the course of subsequent Christian history, there have been Christian communities who once again interpreted Christian tradition as requiring a radical pacifism. Noteworthy among these has been the Society of Friends, known as the Quakers, often successful in aiding victims because of the universal trust inspired by their simple lives and honest dealings. It is one of the misfortunes of history that William Penn's projected experiment of tolerance within Pennsylvania combined with pacifism in relation to the American Indians was cut off prematurely by outside forces. Other Christian groups dedicated to radical pacifism, such as Mennonites, Hutterites, and Brethren, have tended to combine their pacifism with a withdrawal from civic responsibilities in the larger society, isolating themselves in enclaves.

In sum, the arguments against war from the religious traditions are strong and come from many traditions. Moreover, they are practical and practicable and have proved as much in our own times. Nevertheless, these arguments are misted over by some religious endorsements of warlike postures, and some endorsements of specific wars. The strongest argument that can be made is probably the observation that in endorsing wars and threats of war all traditions have expressed their reluctance and their hope that in each case this will reestablish a balance for a lasting peace, while in speaking for pacifism the traditions have drawn their declarations from the very heart of their sacred texts and their established disciplines.

3

Peace, the Tranquility of Order: A Reasonable State

There is general agreement that peace is desirable, even that it is necessary for the fulness of human life in society. Yet again and again whole populations are thrust into war with all its brutalizing sufferings and distortions. Besides greed, selfishness, and lack of empathy with those who are seen as outsiders, there are perhaps three very central reasons for the repetition of wars: the misapprehension that security lies in the power to bully others; the conviction that peace is not really possible in this world; and the tendency to think of peace simply as the absence of war.

Peace: Far More Than the Absence of War

The uncritical definition of peace as the absence of war may be one of the main reasons for the renewed outbreak of war. The settlements after World War I stand as a classic reminder of this. The victors sat in judgment over the conquered, took it as evident that the aggression and misdeeds could be attributed to the conquered side, and proceeded to apply "sanctions" (which were in fact simply punishments visited on whole populations, including children yet unborn), without serious consideration of what that would do to the balance of life in the European society and economy. Moreover, World War I itself was in some measure the outcome of the "peace

33

settlement" after the Franco-Prussian War, sparked though the former was by an assassination. Much the same can be said about the Middle East in our own time and about a number of Third World conflicts in which the absence of declared war by no means indicates that grievances and hostilities have been resolved.

Commonsense observation of history and reflection upon it suggests that peace is far more than the absence of war, and it has a positive content which must be cultivated or constructed. People find themselves in a world in which many resources and opportunities are limited, and in which individuals, groups, and nations are in competition for access to land, mineral deposits, waterways, vegetation and goods made from it, animals and products derived from them, access to outer space, to airwaves, and much else. Moreover, people find themselves in the midst of many self-determining, spontaneously acting, creatively busy beings just like themselves, each of whom has ideas, appetites, and preferences for the distribution of resources and tasks, the pattern of social interaction, laws to govern society, opportunities, and so forth. When all these free-willed individuals are trying to establish themselves in the same universe of activity and life, their inherent capacity for self-determination is doomed to universal and unending conflict in large or small battles of extermination unless they find a way to make a joint project of the exercise of their freedom.

From this simple observation some thinkers, such as the philosopher Thomas Hobbes, have concluded in a pessimistic vein that the natural condition of human beings is a state of universal warfare in which, out of sheer self-defense and instinct for survival, people fashion alliances and eventually build states with laws and machinery to enforce the laws. Others, romantically inclined like Jean Jacques Rousseau, have been more apt to see the "original" or natural state of human beings as idyllic, evading the issue of competing freedoms in the same world. More recently, to those who have held extreme existentialist positions, human freedom is essentially tragic because it is very lonely, existing in a hostile environment, and its promise cannot be fulfilled. Perhaps a more contemporary way to think about the situation of many self-determining beings thrown into a common universe is simply that the "original" or natural state of human beings is unfinished. It calls for active collaboration for its resolution.

All of us are, in fact, constantly busy making a home for ourselves in the world by transforming the physical environment, forging alliances, settling on some predictable patterns for our relationships with one another, producing and distributing what we need to sustain our lives, accumulating funds of knowledge, understanding, and wisdom to deal with all the circumstances that arise. We are never in a finished world, so that any balance or equilibrium in human society has to be a balance in movement and change, not the equilibrium of a state of rest. There are bound to be adjustments and experimentation, and momentary imbalances to be corrected. This means that there is no such phenomenon as the perfect society, in need of no further change. There is necessarily a process of struggle and readjustments. But the question arises concerning optimum conditions and considerations which might bring about true peace.

The answer to the question of what factors and conditions constitute true peace depends largely on what we consider to be a truly happy and fulfilled human life. Many dictatorships have assumed that tight control with consequent predictability and smooth functioning of the state yields peace because people know where they stand and can rely upon the working of the machinery of society. But this quite misses the human desire to participate in shaping one's social life, to exercise choices, experiment, act on one's own evaluations. Other regimes and political philosophies have assumed that there will be true peace if all have adequate access to material goods, only to find that people want more. They want freedom to choose where to live, whether and how to worship, how to raise their children, how to earn their living, and how to spend their money, to mention just a few of the freedoms for which people will start wars or rebellions and riots.

Components of a Peaceable Society

Both Marxist and western democratic traditions have assumed that it is not the business of the state or even of society at large to define what constitutes true human happiness and fulfillment. The task of structuring the social and economic relations within the society is certainly a task of constructing peace, but this is done by providing conditions which allow all in their own way to pursue happiness and fulfillment. That means, of course, laws and sanctions which prevent some from seeking their fulfillment at the expense of others. Both Marxist and western democratic theory has generally supposed that this involves the art of compromise because people will want to pursue goals which are incompatible with one another. Even in the simple society of a family or a college dormitory some members may want to play loud rock music while others want to concentrate on tasks which require quiet, or may simply want to sleep. Even in the most idyllic village some homestead locations are more desirable than others. In any country, as well as in the world as a whole, some regions have more natural resources than others, and some are healthier places to live than others, while again some have easy access to oceans or trade routes which are denied to others. It has long been recognized, therefore, that mathematical equality of possessions and opportunities is impossible in the real world. Indeed, Marxism has acknowledged this also, in spite of some facile stereotypes which have been raised as accusations against that political philosophy. But if absolute equality is not possible, not even absolute equality of opportunity, and if the nature of their happiness and fulfillment is not to be denied or prescribed for people by the regulatory structures of the society, a further understanding is necessary to establish what constitutes a peaceable society. This has several components one of which is personal in the values and expectations of each individual, and this will be considered in chapters 7 and 8. Another component has to do with structures for implementation at the national and international level, and this will be touched upon in chapter 9. This present chapter is concerned with trying to establish what must be the functional categories for a pluralistic nation and a pluralistic world because that is the situation in which we live in our times, and it can be expected to be the human situation for the foreseeable future.

Any proposal for a peaceable society is necessarily proposing an ideal to be striven for, rather than a non-negotiable minimum to be taken for granted because, given existing injustices and sufferings in the world, the minimum that must be taken for granted is quite inadequate to the task of constructing peace. The minimum that is taken for granted in western democracies (though sometimes nevertheless not observed) is a guarantee of physical safety from violence for all individuals, of security of possessions from theft and vandalism, of protection against invasion of the privacy of one's home, an opportunity for a fair trial when accused of breaking the law, and so forth. Careful reflection, however, shows that while these guarantees seem to express a certain level of justice and of law and order, they leave many potential grievances unaddressed. They are negative; they are designed to maintain the existing order without reference to the problem that some may be excluded from the benefits which are being defended, and for the most part they protect the privileged and advantaged against incursions into their privilege by the disadvantaged. It is not unusual to hear the claim that nevertheless our society offers equality of opportunity, so that the underprivileged are so by their own fault. But this is patently untrue because the equality of opportunity is only at best an equality under the law, and even this may not work so well in practice as in theory, as is demonstrated in the United States by the statistics of the racial differential in criminal sentencing, job promotions, and other fields.

Basic Questions of Justice and Inclusion

A number of basic questions of justice and inclusion are, for instance: the right to eat adequately, to be housed with respect for human dignity and health, to have access to adequate medical care in case of need and for routine care such as vaccinations, to have employment opportunities according to one's talents and achievements and at a rate of remuneration which offers at least a living wage for oneself and one's dependents. People will not easily be persuaded that they are living the good life and have no grievances against society while these very basic needs are unmet through no fault of those who suffer the deprivation. And in these circumstances there is no real peace because peace exists where there are no grievances or where grievances are being met as they arise and are made known. In fact, in our western democracies it is only those countries which have embraced some degree and some style of socialism that have addressed the root question about what people can expect from their society in meeting their basic needs as well as the secondary question about how the well-being they enjoy is to be protected against incursions. From experience of trying to establish a society with a peaceable balance, many western European countries, as well as Canada, Australia, New Zealand, and some of the struggling newly independent countries of the Third World, have come to accept the positive demands of constructing a society that meets the needs of all, as well as the negative or restraining demands to protect the goods that people have.

Modern history has amply demonstrated that where basic human needs are not met by the structures within a nation, there is no real peace, and riots, street violence, vandalism, and other destabilizing events can be expected. But what can be said for the internal functioning of one nation can also be said for regional or world affairs. In modern times there has been a rather reluctant acceptance of a certain minimal international law, regulating such matters as fishing rights, air space, passports and visas, some arrangements for disease control, diplomatic immunity, treatment of prisoners of war, etc. All of these regulations deal with matters which are potentially explosive, and it is therefore an important measure towards peace to continue and multiply such arrangements. Moreover, there is some machinery for arbitration and adjudication in place that could be used even to avoid wars, but so far the most powerful nations, and especially the United States, have not been willing to submit their own disputes to the machinery of the United Nations and the International Court. What this has really meant is that the powerful nations have wanted to maintain their dominance by force or the threat of it. This suggests that they are well aware that other peoples have grievances which in a neutral court would be held as justified grievances.

Peace and International Order

In the international sphere as in the national, the achieving of genuine peace depends on an international order in which the basic human needs of all people are being met. A structure of genuine social justice on a worldwide basis is needed, and this will certainly come into conflict with the short-term economic interests of the wealthy and powerful nations. As has been shown many times in this century, economies which are heavily involved in arms production foster war in two ways, by providing the tempting means for a quick advantage in any conflict that may arise, and by drawing off resources needed to meet basic human needs directly or indirectly. In fact, what has happened in our times is that the wealthy and powerful nations have initiated wars when they felt their strategic or economic advantages were threatened, and the poor and smaller nations have initiated wars when they felt that their survival was threatened, whether economically or in terms of a cultural heritage and preferred way of life.

The question of some level of equal rights, and of a pattern of exchanges which meet the basic needs of all is a difficult one. It is not difficult for reasons of world scarcities; research has shown that the fertility of the earth yields enough food, clothing, and shelter for all. It is not difficult for reasons of communication and technology: we have achieved sophisticated and adequate ways of analyzing needs and potentials and adapting processes to implement the necessary production and distribution. It is difficult because those of us who possess relative wealth and power and luxury are not willing to retrench in the interests of those who do not. And because explicitly or implicitly we know this, we tend to project hostility onto others even where it does not exist, and we quickly label it unjust aggression when it does exist. But it would only be unjust if the existing balance of power and wealth in the world were just. It is clear that we shall not have world peace until we have dealt with the grievances that so many peoples rightly harbor, and there is no way to deal with those grievances but by challenging or renouncing some of the advantages of the dominant groups.

Even though we are discussing what should be the ideal conditions in the world for peace, there will be some who will argue that people have all kinds of perceptions of what would constitute a just and peaceable order in the world, and that there is no way of judging between them. It will be argued that the "haves" always want to keep, and the "have nots" to take, and that it is probably better for society on the whole to protect the existing order of things. The persuasiveness of this argument is that it is usually being made by those who have the power to enforce it. Its weakness is that it leaves society always ready to explode into riots or wars.

Rawls' Justice as Fairness Theory

This response, however, does raise the question whether by reason alone we can arrive at some principle of a just society which would constitute a condition for peace. Ethicists, philosophers, statesmen, and others have debated this and offered theories, of which perhaps the most persuasive is the refinement of the "social contract" theory in the form of the "justice as fairness" theory of John Rawls.[7] It is a proposal that deserves careful reflection by all. It proposes as foundation a hypothetical council of all human beings prior to their incorporation into the world. At this council or consultation, the imaginary participants would be in full possession of their mature reasoning power, and they would understand the conditions of life in the world, but they would not know what role they were to play, where and to whom they would be born, what talents they would have, what opportunities would unfold before them, what wealth and power they might expect to command, which sex they would be, and so forth. All these people would be anticipating a great lottery in which their placement in the world would be determined. In this imaginary council before the lottery, they are agreeing on the rules by which their lives on earth will be regulated: criteria for distribution of land, goods, and opportunities; arrangements for dealing with disasters such as droughts and floods and earthquakes; provisions for unemployment, sickness, premature bereavement, etc.; relations between races, ethnic and linguistic groups, peoples of naturally rich lands and of barren lands, those in densely populated areas and those in lands that could support a much larger population, and so forth. Rawls himself did not actually fill in these particular items for consideration, and anyone can apply the theory by filling in further lists. The point of the exercise of imagination and ingenuity proposed by Rawls is that we can indeed come to the most reasonable assessment of what is just in laws, relationships, distribution of goods, etc., by considering what arrangements we would make if a subsequent lottery might put us into the least advantageous position in the situation under consideration.

Although this theory does not give a cut-and-dried answer to specific questions, it provides some necessary keys to finding an answer: justice is more evident from a neutral position; the way to justice and peace requires an exercise of empathy into the situation and experience of others; justice only yields peace if it is all-embracing, inclusive; distortions of justice, which are dangerous to peace, are most likely to happen against the interest of the least powerful and the poorest. This suggests a reasonable way of trying to find that tranquility of order which is true peace. It leaves much to be considered about the quest for peace in a world distorted by consequences of past injustices (which will be attempted in chapters 5 and 6), and need for further reflection on what the religious traditions have to offer on the nature of peace (which is the subject to be considered next, in chapter 4).[8]

4

Peace, the Divine Gift

On three points the great religious traditions of the world are clearly united: peace is divinely ordained or commanded to human beings and human societies; at the same time, peace is a precious gift of heaven because human beings are so persistently quarrelsome; and, finally, peace among nations and groups, as well as among individuals, is directly dependent upon the inner peace of all with their own being and with the ultimate ground and source of their own being, the divine. The religions introduce a new dimension. For them, peace is not only the way reasonable people ought to arrange things and a tranquility of order to be attained and maintained in an unfinished world of flux and surprises. To the eyes of faith, peace belongs to the process and the goal of salvation from sin or exile, from unreality or non-being.

Concept of Shalom

In the biblically based faiths this is made quite clear by the centrality given to the concept of *shalom* (peace, wholeness, well-being), which features prominently in the Hebrew Scriptures, the teaching of Jesus in the Gospels, and the Qur'an. This concept of *shalom*/peace is not defined as the absence of war, but is given a meaning contextually that provides solid positive content. Peace is a condition of security, of belonging, of contentment and fulfillment, of pleasant and sustaining relationships with all, of constructive and purposeful activity, of mutual service and encouragement free from undue stress and anxiety. All this is made possible and, so to speak, held together by the powerful, unifying force of the divine creativity, accepted and reflected in human creativity that remains in full communion with the divine.

The biblical anthropology, or vision of the human, is rigorously realistic, however, in acknowledging that this state of *shalom*/peace is not what exists in the world, but rather what ought to exist, and what, on the conviction that God is a benign and powerful creator, can therefore be realized. In some passages of the Psalms, and of the Wisdom literature generally, there is reflection on this of an analytical or abstract type, but the anthropology of the Bible is expressed most explicitly and forcefully in story form, especially in the early chapters of Genesis.

Unity of God as the Ultimate

In reading stories of origin in any tradition, including the biblical, it is important to realize that the storytellers had no intention of claiming to present chronicles of long-past events based on historical or scientific research. They clearly intended to present an interpretation and analysis of the human situation and human experience in the continuing present which includes all of us in every generation. Thus the stories given in the first three chapters of Genesis, though they appear to give two different accounts of how everything in the world began, are actually suggesting to the interpretive function of the imagination two approaches to an understanding of the coherence and purposefulness and underlying harmony of all that is. Most importantly, these stories insist that there is one all-powerful, benign source and sustaining provider of all that is, the Lord God, and that it is the unity of God as the ultimate that guarantees the possible harmony and unity of all that is called into existence by that God. The unity of God implies unified laws or principles by which all things are harmoniously interdependent and mutually supportive. Moreover, the stories proclaim, the human consciousness is made receptive to the wisdom of God expressed in creation, so that we can discern the laws and principles of creation.

These are certainly implications of the deceptively simple stories in which the Lord God calls for light and order out of a watery chaos, building up a world and universe in which all things have their boundaries and their courses, or in which the Lord God gives water and human beings to barren desert for cultivation and fertility. The added story of the Garden of Eden provides an opportunity for the storyteller to comment on the conditions for harmony which have been built into the creation: a divine prerogative of being at the center and providing the basic wisdom, the life, and the determination of good and evil—in the incident of the tree of life and the tree of the knowledge of good and evil at the center of the garden which must not be snatched and appropriated by human beings. The consequences of such appropriation which are spelled out are insightful: fear of nakedness (vulnerability); estrangement from animals and vegetation, which have become hostile and resistant to order; exile from the pristine harmony of human existence in a good and hospitable environment; estrangement from one another as told later in the Cain and Abel narrative; and the great sorrow of God over the rift in the divine creation.

God's Plan and the Cooperation of People

The recital of how God's wisdom was not observed and shared but rather contested by human beings shows the realism of the biblical faith expressed. Common sense observation indicates that the world and its inhabitants do not enjoy the harmonious, hospitable, and therefore profoundly peaceful existence that seems to be offered to them by nature and human endowments. The explanation for this, according to the biblical wisdom, is that God's plan in creation would work well enough, but it depends on the wholehearted cooperation of human beings for its fullest realization, and that cooperation is being withheld by the inclination to put oneself at the center instead of God. When thousands upon thousands attempt each to put self at the center of planning, organization of society, and fulfillment of needs, there is in effect no center. Believers in the biblical traditions have been made keenly aware of this as regards their individual lives and wants, but are much less aware that the same is true of groups and collectivities such as families, interest groups, races, nations, and even Churches. While striving to be unselfish in individual private life, many devout and good people do not see a contradiction in national policies of domination and enrichment at the expense of other nations, or business promotion at the expense of workers, consumers, environment, future resources, etc. The history of the West and indeed of the world is resonant also with religious imperialism and rivalry between Churches and religious groups. Though it may not be so immediately evident, these collective snatchings of the divine prerogative of being the center also contradict the basic insights of the biblical anthropology. Wars result because the divinely intended harmony has already been destroyed before war was declared. It has been destroyed by the commonly accepted definitions of national sovereignty and by the commonly accepted idea that the responsibility of governments is to their own nation, no matter what their policies may do to other nations. On these principles we cannot have a coherent world, and the biblical wisdom points to self-centeredness and consequent lack of empathy as the sin which lies at the root of the problem.

The biblical foundation stories in Genesis do not end with the sorrow of God and the exile of human beings, but with the assurance that the power and compassion of God is greater than the rift. Salvation is possible and promised if only human beings will respond in the second instance to the divine sharing of the wisdom rejected in the first instance, by which each can attain ultimate happiness and the world can live in hope of restored harmony. This promise of restored harmony echoes through the Scriptures, always with the condition of a return to the One God, the one who is at the center and whose creative word is the law of all that is. Poetically expressed, the nations will study war no more and will come in pilgrimage to Jerusalem; people will beat their swords into ploughshares and their spears into pruning hooks (Isa 2:4).

Peace Requires Repentance and Conversion

What is at the root of the biblical promises of peace and well-being for all is the conviction that peace carries a price. The price is repentance and conversion, both of individuals and of social structures and units. It has been a popular defense of existing inequities and oppression to say that structures and collectivities do not sin, only individuals do; likewise structures and collectivities are not called to repent and be converted, only individuals are. This is not the biblical perspective in which whole nations are called upon to fast and do penance, whole nations are blamed and see in their conquest and despoliation the collective punishment by God of their unjust structures and policies. Deep, therefore, in the wisdom of the biblical traditions is a sense that faith and obedience involve the collectivity and its laws, customs, and structures, as well as the individual. And pervasive in the biblical teachings is the understanding that *shalom*/peace is at one and the same time a gift and a commandment of God, and that it involves radical transformations in human expectations, values, and behavior.

Clearly, all three of the major traditions which are biblically based have deviated spectacularly from this basic insight. Obedience to God's commands has been invoked as the reason for initiating wars which were undeniably wars of aggressive expansion, not of defense. And in so-called wars of national defense, it has frequently been not only survival and homes which have been defended, but commercial and strategic interests in maintaining dominance over other parts of the world or other peoples. Yet the admittedly wretched history of these wars must be set in the context of the protests against them in the name of the same faith—a protest that has frequently come from those in a more neutral position, who were therefore better placed to read the meaning of the tradition with a clear eye.

In the history of Israel there may be many stories of battles wreaking great violence and destruction, but progressively the tradition interprets them as battles with "principalities and powers," the great battle between good and evil, between the creativity of God and the destructiveness of chaos resisting God. Moreover, examples of non-violent and merciful actions yielding peace are also to be found, as in the treatment of the Syrian soliders in 2 Kings 6:8-23, and in the Northern Kingdom's treatment of the southern prisoners in 2 Chronicles 28:6-15. Later in the tradition, in the *Talmud* and the *Midrash Rabbah*, there are many sayings focusing on peace as an imperative, an all-embracing good, and a gift of God to those who live by the Law of God. A moment of reflection on the horrors of destruction of an enemy is inserted into the heart of the Passover Seder (which might otherwise be in danger of being interpreted in a triumphalist sense) when the spilt wine recalls the sorrow of God over the drowned Egyptians.

Gospels: A Handbook for Peacemaking

In the history of Christianity there are terrible wars of conquest, as well as many wars disingenuously justified as wars of defense or of vindication of the oppressed of another nation. But the classic source for Christianity, the Gospels of the New Testament, could be read as a handbook on non-violence and peacemaking. Throughout Christian history there has been a strongly pacifist strand of interpretation of the demands of Christian faith in public life. Moreover, it should be noted that the so-called "just war" theory never proposes war as intrinsically acceptable. From St. Augustine of Hippo in the early fifth century to Reinhold Niebuhr and other "realist" Christian ethicists in the twentieth century, those who proposed such a theory admitted two presuppositions: Jesus himself was pacifist and taught that the way to overcome evil was by doing good, so that any condoning of warfare compromises his teachings; and those who settle for this compromise do so because they are convinced that the complexity and changed circumstances of their own times make it impossible to prevent war, so that it becomes necessary rather to limit it in any way that remains possible. In other words, this is not really a theory to justify warfare, but a theory to limit and restrain it as much as possible when war seems inevitable. The corollary of the theory is a Christian obligation of peacemaking, that is of changing the circumstances in which war appears as inevitable.[9]

The Gospel of Jesus Christ does not really consider compromises but focuses on the radical steps needed in human life and human relationships in order that God's reign which constitutes the ultimate peaceable kingdom may be fully realized. That is why the famous Sermon on the Mount in the Gospel of Matthew seems to many Christians too idealistic to be practical. However, one might turn the tables by suggesting that in a world of so much suffering and violence only the radical is practical in the long run. In that sermon, one of the beatitudes, which function as a kind of platform of the policies Jesus proposes for his followers, is the declaration that peacemakers are acknowledged by God as in some special way the children of God. This suggests that they are truly about the "Father's" business in their peacemaking, collaborating with the Creator to bring about in the second instance the harmony and joy that was lost in the first by the seizing of the center which is the divine prerogative. What becomes very clear in the New Testament is that the peace which is seen as a gift of God and which Jesus Christ gives to his followers is not a state but a process. The issue is one of discernment and cooperation in the adjustment and transformation of human values and expectations and relationships, and Jesus himself warns that the process cannot be other than conflictual, but must be non-violent. This implies an understanding of peace which embraces justice and truth—the truth of the human situation before God and in relation with one another and with the rest of creation.

Muslims and the Quest for Peace

Christians often assume that the passion for peace which is at the heart of the Gospel is not shared by others, and particularly not by Muslims. This is really an inadvertent slander of the Islamic tradition. Muslims, like Jews, are very concerned to achieve the peace in society that comes of submission to God and to the Law of God. Although they acknowledge a revelation which Jews and Christians do not accept, that is the Qur'an as received by the Prophet Muhammad, the underlying theme is submission to God as the one and only means of achieving not only personal salvation but also peace on earth for all peoples. Therefore one of the obligations acknowledged by a Muslim is *jihad,* or striving, and it is expressed in many practices in the personal and social life of a Muslim. The common western interpretation of *jihad* as meaning "holy war," that is war of conquest and territorial expansion in the name of Allah, is simply not a correct translation. Like Jews and Christians, Muslims have fought wars of expansion and have done things in those wars which are incompatible with the pure spirit and teaching of Islam. But like Christians, Muslims have an explicit "just war" theory, that is a well-developed teaching which limits war in many ways—the reasons for which a war may be fought if injustices cannot otherwise be put right, the necessity of making all possible attempts at peaceful negotiations first, the prohibition against attacking non-combatants or those who are already fleeing from the battle, and many further restrictions. Because of the popular image that we have formed in the West of Muslims as intrinsically warlike and self-righteously so, it seems very important that this bias for peace and rejection of war in Islam should become better known among Christians. A noteworthy example of it is the life and leadership of Abdul Ghaffar Khan, who had learned nonviolence not from Gandhi but from his own Muslim father.[10]

On factor that is common, then, to all the biblical traditions is that peace is God-given and can only be received on God's terms. A second common factor is the understanding that peace requires a deep conversion of the individual and a concomitant conversion of the structures of society to God's wisdom for creation; it cannot be achieved by leaving the accepted norms of public life as they are. A third common factor is the realization that in spite of obstacles and betrayals, peace in this deepest sense remains both promise and commandment; the biblical message calls for peacemakers in all circumstances, no matter how discouraging.

Passion for Peace and the Non-biblically Based Religions

The religious passion for peace, and the religious insight into the true and comprehensive nature of peace is by no means limited to the biblically based religions, but can be found in all the traditions. As already mentioned in chapter 2, Hindu tradition with its various offshoots into Buddhism, Jainism, and some other newer forms, developed the posture of *ahimsa*, or non-harming, to a high and sophisticated degree, especially in the ascetical development of the individual. An aspect that these traditions have in common with the biblical ones is the realization that a right and peaceable social order is not something that human beings can invent out of their own ideas or preferences but something that is inherent in the universe and must be discovered by communion with the depths of being.[11] Thus they acknowledge, though with quite different symbolism, the gift quality of peace among human individuals, classes, races, and nations. Another aspect which these traditions share in a marked way with the Christian is the understanding that peace necessarily involves some renunciation or self-sacrifice in order to transcend existing tensions, conflicts of interest, and hostilities.

The fruit of that traditional wisdom became a precious legacy to the whole world through its implementation by the Mahatma Gandhi.[12]

In Buddhism and Jainism, and to a less marked degree in Hinduism, the commitment to non-violence, and its underlying concept of world harmony and peace among peoples, is more comprehensive than in the western religions because it includes all sentient creatures. There is a deep sense of fellowship with living beings, and of the interdependence of all beings in the world.[13] This sensitivity, which is found also in the traditions of the Amerindians, is something that may be well for western societies to learn and cultivate because it has implications for the development of that kind of empathy which is an indispensable element of peace-making, and also because such sensitivity responds to the ecological crises in which we now find ourselves, and which in turn have a strong impact on the creation of peace among nations.

To be realistic, one must recognize that like ourselves of the West, the peoples of India saw centuries of warfare even before the British came, in spite of the strong ascetic traditions of *ahimsa*. But in this they are like all the peoples of the earth; they hand on teachings of true wisdom which are not always honored in practice but are nevertheless honored in theory and accepted in principle. Such a tradition of wisdom is not useless in human history. Simply by being accepted in principle, such wisdom holds out an invitation from generation to generation which some few people in the community will take seriously and revitalize by their example and by their impact on institutions.

Ahisma *and* Karma

A further characteristic of the various Indian traditions in their teaching of *ahimsa* is that as an ascesis for the individual it is closely linked to the notion of *karma*, a moral law of cause and effect. Just as the biblically based religions expect human persons to be rewarded or punished by God either in the present life or in an afterlife as an outcome of their past behavior, so the Indian traditions assign moral responsibility and consequences. Hinduism gives a certain rigorous logic to the idea of *karma* by applying it to the understanding that souls transmigrate from body to body, life after life, finding themselves in each case in a condition that is the outcome of behavior in previous lives. In this context, killing and every kind of violence are destructive of those who commit them, and the reverse is also true; the practice of *ahimsa* is ennobling and enhancing of the future existence of the doer.

There is a kind of ethic of virtue implied: non-violence makes us better and happier people. This seems to offer a close correspondence with the gospel-derived spirituality of the beatitudes, and to provide a significant common ground for peacemaking activities and movements.

Buddhism and Non-violence

Buddhism, since its inception, has preached non-violence and peace as its message to all peoples for all situations. It has also taught from the beginning a nuanced and profoundly spiritual understanding of the nature of peace. This is perhaps best illustrated by some of the stories passed on about what the Buddha did and said. In his own earthly days he protested against the harsh punishments meted out to malefactors and the harsh reprisals against enemies, on the grounds that hatred cannot overcome hatred and violence cannot end violence. He contended that crime and territorial aggression would be ended if a decent means of earning a livelihood and reasonable living conditions were provided for all. It would then be possible for people to live without fear or anxiety and there would be no incentive to violence and lawlessness, and therefore the realm would enjoy peace. Advising lay people on how to find true happiness, the Buddha urged them to develop skill in their profession or trade and to practice it energetically and with dedication; to use and store resources prudently, and to live well within their income; to cultivate good, sensible, faithful friends; and to be generous with those in need and with good works for the community.[14]

Similarly, it is told of the Buddha that he taught that wars among nations were not necessary for defense or for redress of injuries, and that on at least two occasions in his life he demonstrated this by his personal intervention, even walking right onto the battlefield, to settle peacefully a dispute between the Sakyas and the Koliyas in one case and between King Ajatasattu and the Vajjis in the other case. It may be worth noting in passing that the same is told of St. Elizabeth of Portugal in the Christian tradition. Although the Buddha left remarkably practical and sagacious criteria for good government, the main point of the Buddhist teaching on peace seems to be that where individuals are at peace within themselves, they will also create peaceful societies. This personal peace is based on universal love and compassion for all living beings, supported by the mental discipline of clear awareness and full concentration, and likewise guided by the wisdom shaped by a certain selflessness in detachment and by non-violent thoughts.

What is significant here is the understanding of the close intertwining of inner and outer peace, and the realization that peace is a process, a discipline reaching far beyond the absence of physical aggression. This also corresponds closely to the understanding expressed in the words of Jesus in the Sermon on the Mount, that the problem does not begin with killing but with the harboring of anger and contempt in one's heart (Matt 5:21-22).

Confucian Traditions and Peace

The Confucian traditions of China also offer some significant common ground for an understanding of peace, though there is always a question whether this should be thought of as a religious or a philosophical tradition. Confucius had to face the problem of wars and violence in an urgent way in his own time because a network of brutal local wars was tearing apart the fabric of society. His contention was that society is not held together in peaceful interaction by external force but by forces working from within people. In particular, he thought that a fully conscious tradition had to be built and maintained by diligent cultivation, based on respect for the dignity of each person including oneself, civility in all dealings between people, propriety (prescribing relationships such as filial piety), moral authority in leadership, and the cultivation of the arts of peace (fine arts). It is clear that these foundations for a peaceful society require a constant personal asceticism and involve a considerable degree of self-restraint in always placing the common good above self-interest.[15]

What appears as an ethical and extremely practical teaching in the Confucian tradition also finds a corresponding mysticism in Taoism, the way of the universe, the benign harmony in which human lives can and should also be blended. Tao is a way of peace, followed by putting self aside and transcending all disturbing emotions by such exercises as breath control and meditation, or alternatively pursued by attentive study of the harmony of the universe and a blending of oneself into it. The teachings of the Tao tradition maintain that this activates a power that can withstand the force of arms non-violently, leading to the movement that called itself the Way of Great Peace. Though this has sometimes been popularly interpreted as a mysterious era of peace to come in the future, it rests on the long-standing practice of *wu-wei*, a kind of radical non-violence, seeking to be in tune with the Tao in simplicity in all one's actions, and referring to all aspects of personal and public life in the historical present.[16]

Peace and the Baha'i and the Unification Church

This chapter would not be complete without mentioning the especially strong peace bias in the more recently founded religious traditions, such as the Baha'i and the Unification Church. These movements place world peace and the harmonious wellbeing of all peoples at the heart of their endeavors, both in the outreach of the communities and in the personal lives and relationships of their members. Keenly aware that religions have often been used as the pretext for conquests and wars and persecutions, these newer traditions focus on the need for peace among the religions themselves. In conclusion, it may be said that the basis for such peace and for fruitful collaboration of religions in the pursuit of peace is clearly already there in the classic teachings of the various traditions.

5

Peace Has Its Logic: A Reasonable Quest

The degree to which we achieve peace in the world is a matter within the scope of human freedom, though it is a very complex matter because of the multiplicity of individual human freedoms involved and because of the increased difficulty of collaboration in very large social structures. Such structures become cumbersome, very susceptible to manipulation in some ways and for some purposes, but at the same time extremely resistant to transformation in other ways for other purposes. Consequently, many people, even in well-developed democracies, of long standing and proven stability, have a sense of helplessness, of not counting, of being in the grasp of impersonal forces working according to laws of their own which subordinate human freedom.

This is a very dangerous attitude. People may not actually have as much freedom in particular cases as they think they have, but this is a problem which is self-correcting, for they come up against their limits and learn by necessity what these limits are. However, it is also true that people do not have more freedom than they think they have because the freedom they do not exercise is not effectively in their possession. And this is not a self-correcting problem. It requires an outside stimulus to bring such people to awareness of their greater freedom. This is the perennial problem of slave or oppressed consciousness. It is not confined to those living in daily physical fear, utter deprivation, or deliberately contrived ignorance and isolation; it is a very common situation of many otherwise intelligent and competent people in the large contemporary democracies, and it is a threat to justice and peace and to the economy and ecology of the world.[17]

Yet the making of world peace requires a pervasive sense of responsibility and of power among world populations. None of us can achieve this for other peoples, but all of us can begin within our own context and find ways of widening circles of collaboration. Many efforts at such networks exist, and some of these are listed in an appendix to this book. The purpose of this chapter is to explore what may be called the fundamental logic of human peacemaking.

Desirability of Peace

The logic of peacemaking begins with the desirability of peace. No one chooses war for its own sake but for the sake of some other perceived good. This may be a true good, like the liberation of an oppressed people, the defense of one's home and civilization from attack, or the rescue of hostages or other prisoners. Or it may be perceived as good but not actually be so, like the promotion of arms sales, an industrial complex dependent upon such sales, the maintenance of channels for sale of health-threatening addictive drugs, or the control of superior bargaining power in commercial exchanges designed to keep dependent nations subservient and impoverished. But whether war is fought for a true good or for one falsely perceived as good, it is not fought for its own sake. From this it follows that if the same end can be shown to be attainable without war, this would ordinarily be preferred, other factors like expense being equal. Similarly, if something perceived as good but not truly good can be shown to be destructive and as such eliminated within one's own society, this cause for war would have ended. Of course, this is a highly simplified and abstract scheme. It abstracts from situations in which certain unscrupulous interest groups are manipulating the majority, often by concealing the true nature of claims and proposals. It also abstracts from the practical difficulties in shaping common values and expectations in large pluralist societies. Nevertheless, attempts to discern, understand, and share reasonable approaches to peace are never lost. Cumulatively, all such efforts have their effect in shaping the attitudes and expectations of the society.

Security in Mutual Trust

Taking the first principle, the universal desirability of peace, as established, and likewise its corollaries, namely, that given equal chances of success, people will choose means other than war, and that persuaded the goals are not truly good, the country will not support a war, one can see the next reasonable steps in peacemaking more clearly. Each country or bloc is more secure when all know that their legitimate pursuit of truly good goals can be achieved by means other than war. Again the principle is self-evident and deceptively simple in the abstract. In practice it involves general agreement on what are truly good goals, and these need to be defined in the context of coexistence in the world with all the other groups. In the real world this may seem like an impossible task. For example, for about half a century the general population of the United States, and in a lesser degree some of its allies, were quite easy in conscience with the judgment that saving people from communist rule, or even influence, was such a great good that it justified the infliction of immense loss of life, terrible personal injuries both to fighters and to civilian populations, massive destruction of forests and crops with chemicals that poisoned the future for the local people, destruction of traditional social structures, organization of assassination of heads of state, creation of terrible refugee problems for generations to come, and much else. Meanwhile for many decades there was an assumption in the Soviet bloc that the great good for which all these same things might be inflicted on certain vulnerable populations was the introduction of a truly just society for the future through a radically socialist transformation. And during those decades many poor populations of the Third World became poorer, and some were totally destroyed.[18]

Now that the worst of the Cold War is over, there is a time of opportunity to return to some very basic considerations of what is truly good for all. Whenever the question is raised explicitly, there is general agreement that survival of populations free from famine and disease, as well as from deaths by violence, is a basic good to which all ought to be able to lay claim. More and more in the contemporary world there is also more or less worldwide agreement that political democracy, in which all adults can participate directly or indirectly in shaping the laws and social structures of society, is a desirable goal for every country but cannot be imposed on any country by the specifications of outsiders. Less generally agreed is the further principle that economic democracy is desirable or even possible. Competitive appropriation into private hands of larger and larger accumulations of the means of production at the expense of the dispossessed who become less and less able to compete for a livelihood is a process that is still taken as inevitable and acceptable in most of the world. Yet it is over this issue that the greatest conflicts build up, not between the economically powerful and the dispossessed, but among already powerful contenders for even greater competitive advantages.

Distinguishing a Good to Be Pursued

This brings us back to the problem of distinguishing what is truly a good to be pursued and what only seems so. There are two widely different approaches to this. One is basically the approach that what I want and can "get away with" is good, and that the goods of various competitors in a society are necessarily going to go to those who compete hardest, which is neither good nor bad as an arrangement, but simply the way things inevitably are. But this is clearly not a peace-seeking approach, and it can be challenged on a number of grounds. The other approach is that what promotes life, health, enjoyment, knowledge, wisdom, community bonds, and so forth without thereby depriving or damaging others is good. This obviously is a criterion that can only be applied with study and consultation, tentatively or provisionally, and with a high degree of commitment to the common good above one's individual or interest group's desires and preferences. This is one of the junctures at which peacemaking activities are possible and effective. In general, people are afraid that if they act for the common good and not for their own competitive advantage, some other individual or group will put them at a disadvantage because such others will not be operating by the principle of the common good but by the principle of all-out competition. This anxiety is well based on experience. Therefore action for the common good, whether of individuals or of nations, needs a good deal of support from commonly agreed rules and neutral means of arbitration in disputes. Most people have worked out such rules and procedures within the smaller units of world society, and to some extent up to the national level. Theoretically at least we have such rules and procedures at the international level through the United Nations and through various trading and migration agreements, for instance. But the important question to consider, from a peacemaking point of view, is why these arrangements so frequently fail to be honored in practice.

Any unbiased analysis of the breakdown of arbitration at the international level shows that the strongest countries (economically or militarily or both) judge that it is to their greater advantage to insist on their claims by force, than to risk having them tailored down by an international court or arbitration team. The reason for this is that they consider territorial acquisition, greater material wealth, or domination of other nations more advantageous to themselves than would be the general satisfaction of all parties and all onlookers that justice is being done. The only way the national and international behavior of the powerful nations could be changed is through a transformation of their values and expectations which would give higher worth to community bonds at all levels, and to the security born of trust and friendship at all levels, than to material wealth or bullying power. This seems to be a key point of intervention in the logic of peace and of peacemaking.

Quest for Human Fulfillment: A Community Quest

It is clear that, if the world with its presently known resources is to provide for all, many of us in the wealthier countries need to consume much less of those resources. But that will only happen if people can be brought to seek their happiness in something other than luxury, whether for pleasure or for show, and if they can be brought to respect competence and fairness more than the power to compel by force through monopolies of wealth and killpower. This really means that the quest for true human fulfillment must be seen always as a community quest, and in many of its aspects as a worldwide community quest. It does not mean that all aesthetic, intellectual, linguistic, relational, and religious preferences need to be reduced to uniformity. There is no reason why houses in Japan and in South Africa should be built in the same way or from the same materials, nor why the music of India and of Italy should be the same, but an urgent question arises if some countries or segments of population are homeless in a world full of wealth, or culturally deprived in a world of great opportunities. If cheap food in the United States is being maintained at the cost of abjectly inadequate wages in parts of Latin America, and subhuman conditions of life for migrant farm workers even in the United States, there is an imbalance which no neutral court or arbitration panel will condone. Sooner or later this imbalance will be challenged, be it ever so non-violently, and will be maintained only by the violence of the powerful. Whether this happens within one country or in more complex patterns in the international arena, it is a rupture of peace, which has really begun not with the open violence but with the injustice which preceded it.

Two-pronged Approach to the Logic of Peace

It is clear, therefore, that the logic of peace requires a two-pronged approach: on the one hand the elimination of injustices in society, and of great poverty and mass suffering, and also of desires and striving which are contrary to the common good; and on the other hand, the development and commitment to use peaceful means for the settling of disputes and the hearing of claims. The first requires complex ethical and technical analysis of the issues. While the principle is easy to set forth and to understand, the application involves many social and technical skills. If three or four of us are sitting at a dinner table and one grabs so much of the food that the others rise from the table hungry, it is obvious enough that the satisfaction of the first is at the expense of the others and constitutes an injustice. When the peoples of the earth draw from the resources of the earth for their sustenance and some die of famine in massive numbers, the principle is the same, but it is much more complicated to trace the patterns of causality which link the luxury and waste of some with the starvation of the others. When year after year grain surplus is stored or destroyed in some places, or farmers are paid not to plant, while elsewhere people cannot even survive and children who remain alive grow up brain damaged from malnutrition, there are so many people and economic structures and relationships involved that the chain of causality and responsibility is very elusive.

What is required then, to the extent that peace depends on justice and elimination of destitution, is, among other things, painstaking and detailed economic analysis of the various production, distribution, investment, and transportation patterns by which the food accumulates in one place and the people in the other. Moreover, such studies need to be made with the right questions in mind: not how to maximize profit for the producers, or how to provide cheap consumer goods for just one section of the world population, but rather how to serve the real needs of the whole human community, providing the food needed immediately but also providing for self-sufficiency by home production or exchange in the future, without exhausting soil and resources. Not only is this a very large task, requiring many specialist skills as well as a great deal of data collection, it is also a task that benefits primarily those who cannot afford to sponsor it. It necessarily benefits those who are now being left out or deprived, while research is usually done under the sponsorship of those whose margin of profit is so great that they have the wealth to spare to fund research.

The foregoing suggests that a clearer understanding of those patterns of mass suffering which are caused by extreme poverty needs to be undertaken in the world public interest, sponsored by international groups free of manipulation by wealthy powers in their own interest. This may seem like the impossible, but this is only one step in a process that must go farther. It is also necessary to disseminate the findings and to act upon them, but in this the cooperation of the powerful nations and of the powerful within each nation is required. It is true that large amounts of foreign aid are now being disbursed by the wealthy and powerful countries, but, in addition to the fact that a good deal of it is military aid, much of it is calculated to promote the interests and relative advantages of the donor countries. What is needed, therefore, is quite a significant adjustment in the patterns of foreign aid. This in turn will really only happen if the powerful within the donor countries can be persuaded that it is in the long-term national interest, and in their own long-term or true interest.

Desirable Goals: Apparent or True?

This, however, brings us right back full circle to the problem of what it is that people see as being in their own interest—the question of what goals and desires are truly good and which are only apparent goods, and the even more difficult question of who is to decide this. The elimination of injustices, oppression, and abject poverty of whole populations depends on a correct assessment of the kind of freedom and fulfillment which human beings can properly look for, given our existence of interdependence in society and in a finite universe where the earth must accommodate all of us. Therefore, inevitable in the process of genuine peacemaking is not only the analysis and dissemination of what needs to be done but also much reflection and discussion of how it benefits those who according to their present accepted values appear to be simply the losers by such redress of justice. And this process of transformation can only come about by profound personal changes in the self-identity of individuals, in the satisfactions they seek, in what they experience as good relationships and pleasurable activities—a challenge that will be considered in chapter 7. It is enough to point out here that the motivation for such changes is usually associated with religious conversions. The reasonable logic of peacemaking can point out what is needed but seems to fall considerably short of the target in providing the motivation.

The Technical Side

The other prong of the approach to peacemaking as manifest by the light of reason is perhaps more amenable to purely reasonable approaches. The development of the channels, structures, and processes which offer peaceful ways of settling disputes among nations is the kind of exercise that has built up civilization for millennia and has come to be accepted by human society as a necessary component of life together.

People Are Not Trustworthy Judges in Their Own Cause

It is one of the achievements of western civilization that it has gained universal or almost universal acceptance of the principle that people are not trustworthy judges in their own cause. Courts and legal systems have been built on that principle. Laws and rules must be set down beforehand so that they can be held to apply equally to all as the occasion arises. Moreover, the realization that bias refers not only to one's own cause but to that of anyone more closely allied with oneself than the opponent in the cause has led to the invention of juries, so that a range of perceptions by people selected for their apparent neutrality may be brought to bear on claims and contentions.

The struggle in this century to apply such legal systems and such courts in the international sphere is still quite young. It is true that it has met with obstacles, with efforts to manipulate and with outright refusal to accept rulings. But it is also true that in the long history of western civilization there have been similar struggles to apply the rule of law within nations to those who ruled them, or held men at arms in their command, or wielded great wealth. The reduction of absolute to constitutional monarchies was not achieved without great struggles. Participation in the process of legislation by all adults through elections was only achieved incrementally over long periods of time. Genuine equality under the law was denied to women until very recently, in the United States until recently to almost all people of African ancestry, and in the British Empire to the colonized peoples. All of this, however, has not discouraged those who trust in reasonable ways of regulating society from working constantly to refine and improve the system.[19]

What has been possible within nations with great effort can be expected to be possible among nations with greater effort. The logical argument for this is by analogy. We are not dealing with a totally different situation but with a more complex and larger extension of the same human situation. Just as local chieftains banded into nations and nations into empires, federations, alliances, or power blocs, so the process of aggregation and alliance into common arrangements is likely to continue and can be helped along. One of the reasons for this expectation is the exponential increase in our power of communicating and storing information. The possibility of coordinating efforts and goals for a very large and very scattered population depends in the first place on adequate communications, and these have only very recently developed to produce worldwide instantaneous networks. It is also true that the power of manipulation, and the danger of its being used unscrupulously, is also very great, and extends as widely as the network, which is worldwide. However, the real problems which are likely to pose obstacles are not in the development of the machinery to implement fair dealing in international relations but, again, in persuading those who now have most power that this is a good goal. This in the long term will be beneficial to all, assuring a depth of peace which the world has never really known since the large-scale interchange between various civilizations began. In fact, to a large degree the machinery is in place, and the remaining challenge is to achieve enough consensus to use it and to abide by the decisions made.

Those Most Wanting Peace

There is another aspect to consider in the logic of peace as a reasonable quest. Those who most want peace are those who suffer most from war or from that state of seething hostilities and fears which might as well be war. In the first place that includes refugees, displaced populations, unwanted minorities or immigrants, small nations situated between large warlike powers, ordinary people living in disputed territories, and small nations which happen to have strategically important natural resources. But in the second place it includes all the ordinary people who are worse off whenever there is actual war, or cold war armaments build up. That includes those living in the area where the fighting takes place or where the buildup of kill-power terrifies the inhabitants. It includes all who will feel the pinch of scarcities, and that means most of all the poorest who have fewer ways to compensate for what is lacking. It also includes all those who are likely to be personally involved in fighting or to be targets of bombardment, destruction of homes and fields and other means of livelihood. Most of all, it includes those who will be killed or forever severely handicapped and marginated from ordinary human social and productive pursuits and those who may live the rest of their lives in despair from the memory of what they have seen and what they have been forced to do. In other words, those who least want war or other unresolved hostilities are ordinary people whenever they are aware of what war and hostilities really mean.

Those Most Likely to Want War

Those who are most likely to want war, or to promote cold war hostilities, are those whose personal and family risk is small and whose likely gain in wealth or power from a victory is seen as highly desirable. It is also true, of course, that a whole people can be so ideologically conditioned that they are not free to look at the facts of war and the values that are being balanced against one another. Or it is possible that a whole people may be so certain of victory and so unable to empathize with those of the other side that they see a war as posing scarcely any real risk and assume they themselves will be none the worse for it. Yet when all the possibilities are considered it is evident that ordinary people have usually the most to lose and the least to gain by war and by warlike postures and relationships between nations. Hence, a significant peace-making strategy is to make democracy work better.

Self-interest and Concern for Peace

In most of our large modern democratic systems, many people feel so powerless that they do not exercise the privileges and responsibilities of full citizenship. They understand, rightly, that one vote, one lobbying telephone call or letter, one person attending a town meeting or political rally will make very little difference. It requires both hope and patience, not to mention a great deal of work, to fashion alliances and maintain discussion and pressure, to bring issues to light and discover the extent of popular support for policies and proposals. Unfortunately, self-interest is in practice more successful in engaging people in political activity than altruism. But in the case of ordinary people, especially the poor, self-interest and concern for peace coincide substantially. If these people can be drawn more actively and critically into the democratic process, there is a better outlook for peace. Hence, action to promote the democratic process by information, motivation, and provision of channels and alliances through which ordinary people can have an impact, and can know that they are having an impact, is effectively though indirectly work towards broadening and deepening the peace processes of the world.

In sum, the channels and technical expertise for the reasonable quest for peace are not lacking, but the most significant challenge is in the realm of motivation. It is a challenge to motivate those who have power and see their advantage as lying elsewhere, and it is a challenge to motivate those who know that their advantage lies in justice and peace for all but who are convinced they are powerless to do anything about it.

6

Peace Has Its Price: The Testimony of the Religions

As pointed out in the previous chapter, peacemaking is a complex process, requiring many skills and much work, but the "know-how" for understanding and implementation is well within the scope of human reason. The real obstacles lie elsewhere, not in the ability but in the willingness. Willingness for peace in general or in the abstract is, of course, there. What is not there is the willingness to pay the price for the moves that constitute a thorough structuring of societies and their internal and external relationships for authentic peace. The injustices, aggressions, oppressions, and deprivations which distort societies are always at least apparently of advantage to some group or category of persons who are loath to lose such advantage and therefore doggedly or fiercely resistant to change.[20]

The religions of the world have in various ways come to terms with this, maintaining that the good life requires self-discipline and restraint because the desires of human beings are not spontaneously in order. In particular, most traditions note that people are inclined to want more material goods than they really need and that the acquisition of material goods does not satisfy the desire for them. On the contrary, that desire seems to grow with acquisition. The traditions also observe that modesty and humility do not come spontaneously to people. Rather they are inclined to assert themselves to the detriment of others, and the acquisition of status and prestige do not satisfy the desire for them but tend to make people even more competitive in their need to be honored and preferred. Moreover, it is not only honor but power over others which is at stake, and the wielding of that power tends to be to the detriment of those subjected to it, while further desire feeds and grows on the power already achieved. Besides material possessions, honor and power, pleasure and entertainment have the same seductive and addictive qualities, especially the modern electronic forms of entertainment which, besides promoting themselves, tend to elicit artificial appetites for more material possessions. One factor is common in all of these desires: they are exclusive of the needs or desires of others, in competition with them, and working against community rather than for it, against compassion for the underprivileged or those with grievances.

Perhaps of all the traditions, the Buddhist and the Christian have been the most emphatic about the need to transcend such desires. In the Buddhist tradition this is proposed in the first place for the happiness and deliverance of the individual, but then it becomes a community building factor. In the Christian tradition it is proposed first as required by the Reign of God (an image of the greater social cosmic harmony), and then it becomes more and more a matter of the perfection and happiness of the individual. This order, of course, is in the history of the two traditions, not necessarily in the sequence in which the individual believer in our time encounters the teachings. What is significant is that whether one begins with the individual or with the society, the critical awareness and consequent asceticism proposed is much the same: the discernment and transcending of inauthentic desires.

A Marxist Insight

Before looking a little more closely at the teaching on this matter of these two traditions, it may be helpful to note a corresponding insight from an unexpected direction. Herbert Marcuse of the Frankfurt school, applying Marxist analysis of alienation to American society in the 1960s, found that the alienation and oppression of contemporary Americans no longer fitted the patterns which Marx himself had so movingly described. From his own and others' observations in mid-nineteenth-century Europe, Karl Marx wrote of the dehumanization of dispossessed working people in urban factories. He diagnosed their problems as follows: they were exhausted and crushed by unbelievably long hours of work, but at the end of it were not better off because they did not own what they had produced. Moreover, this labor was boring, bad for their health, and under conditions they would never themselves have chosen. In consequence, what should have been their pride and joy and an extension of themselves, the material world about them was rather something that oppressed them and was experienced as hostile. Finally, instead of having relationships of mutual service in their work, which would have given them the dignity and respect and satisfaction which artists and professional people receive, their working conditions pitted them against one another in ceaseless competition and against their employers in the struggle for a living wage against the pressure of the employer's desire for profit.[21]

Although we hear of conditions in some Third World countries and among some migrant and domestic workers which would answer this description even today, Herbert Marcuse made the point that most people of the western industrialized world are economically oppressed but in such a subtle way that they do not realize it. They are not really oppressed by grim conditions for earning a living or by wretchedly inadequate wages but in their own consciousness which has been and is being unscrupulously manipulated for profit. Through advertising, window displays, the entertainment offered by the media, the character and complexity of goods on the market, people are constantly being persuaded that their happiness depends on more and more possessions of a non-essential kind. Therefore they want more, spend more, must work more hours to pay for it, are burdened by quite unnecessary debts, and are deeply dissatisfied after all. However, they are so persistently brainwashed that they cannot correctly identify the source of their misery. They are persuaded that the problem is that they have not acquired enough or do not have the latest models or the most fashionable variety or whatever has now become prestigious. Therefore, they turn to even more wanting, spending, going into debt, working extra hours, and the whole cycle repeats itself at ever increasing speed, pressure, and suffering. In other words, people look for relief in the very ways that will increase their bondage and anxiety. They do not recognize the true problem which is in the character of the wanting, the nature of the desires, because the things that are wanted cannot by their very nature satisfy the real needs of human beings.[22]

Because this reflection comes out of an avowedly Marxist context, a context heavily committed to the idea that the production of plenty will create the conditions in which people can be more free, more fully human, it is an unexpected confirmation of what religious traditions have taught for millennia. It might almost have been derived directly from either the Buddhist or the Christian tradition. It recognizes a truth that has been noted by religious teachers and by many philosophers: having things, pleasure, prestige, and power does not make people happy. Yet again and again people act on the assumption that it will do so and become addicted to the repetition of what is only bringing them frustration and utter weariness. True wisdom is in the recognition of the contradiction in one's own experience and in attaining to a certain detachment or balance which leads to happiness.

The Buddhist Way

The Buddhist tradition, though expressed in the classic texts in formulations that tend to be rather obscure to people of western experience, speaks of the universal human situation in which all of us find ourselves. It begins at a very deep interior level of human experience with the Four Noble Truths. The first of these is in the recognition of the pervasiveness of a kind of restlessness, frustration, suffering, impermanence, incompleteness, dependence, and vulnerability. The Second Noble Truth is insight into the way such a condition arises, which is "thirst" or craving. Although the teachings of the Buddha are addressed to the individual for the individual's path to enlightenment and personal liberation, the Buddha himself also applied the Second Noble Truth to the affairs of societies and to whole nations, saying that all wars and hostilities come from cravings, from selfish desires, and can only be transcended when the cravings are transcended. The Third Noble Truth is the realization that the suffering, frustration, restlessness can be ended by eliminating the cravings; in other words liberation is possible. Among the explanations of the content of that liberation, the following have been attributed to the Buddha and treasured in the tradition: the extinction of craving, of hatred and of illusion, freedom from pride and the uprooting of attachment. The whole emphasis is on selflessness, a renunciation of central and overriding claims for a discrete and enduring self. In this the Buddhist teaching goes far beyond Christian exhortations to selflessness, but the implications of the Buddhist teaching for community building, harmony, and peace are such as offer most fruitful possibilities of collaboration to Christians.[23]

The completion of the Buddhist insight or enlightenment is in the Fourth Noble Truth: the Middle Path, or the following of the Way that leads to self-transcendence, the end of cravings, hatred, and illusion. The Middle Path between indulgence and asceticism, also known as the Noble Eightfold Path, offers a teaching which addresses all aspects of life, not only for monks but for lay people involved in ordinary affairs of family, business, and public life. From the point of view of world peacemaking, Right Understanding, Right Thought, Right Speech, Right Action, Right Livelihood, Right Effort, Right Mindfulness, and Right Concentration are all interpreted in surprisingly practical ways. The Middle Way is not only a program of self-discipline with one's own liberation in view, but it is described as a way of compassion for all living beings. Thus, Right Speech focuses on truth-telling, on friendly manner and benevolent content, and on speaking only what is useful. Right Action focuses on total honesty, respect for life, chastity, and support for the dignity and good conduct of others. Right Livelihood means making one's living in ways that support a good society and quite explicitly forbids trading in or making lethal weapons, intoxicants, or poisons, or any profession which involves killing or harming. Clearly, such an ethic, lived with sustained commitment by many people, is an effective peace-building process.[24]

In the Middle Way, the psychological component of Right Effort, Right Mindfulness, and Right Concentration is a crucial support or complement to the ethical component just described. To conform one's whole mentality, to become keenly aware of one's own attitudes, feelings, and so forth, and to practice recollection, clarity of focus, simplicity and totality of attention, is from a Buddhist point of view important for its own sake. It is also important, however, in that it makes serious practice of the ethical component possible without self-deception and betrayal. This is further complemented by Right Understanding (seeing things as they really are), and Right Thought (thinking about things non-violently, lovingly, and with a certain selfless detachment), which offer the wisdom component. The implications of this kind of shaping of one's life for public affairs and world peace are obvious: it involves a transcending of nationalism, party factions, feuds and revenge at any level, reliance upon physical force to achieve even good purposes, as well as motives of personal power, wealth, prestige, or any other personal advantage or advancement.[25]

The Reign of God Is the Reign of Peace

Christian readers may be impressed with the realization that although this Buddhist teaching is given in a non-theist context (Buddhists do not worship a supreme God or attempt to relate to a supernatural realm), the convergence with Christian teachings on spirituality is substantial. Though in subsequent centuries Christian teaching has often been reduced in practice to rule-keeping of a rather external kind, there is no trace of this in the recorded teachings of Jesus of Nazareth. All the gospel speeches, sermons, conversations, prayers, and casual sayings of Jesus recorded are concerned with the need for a radical reshaping of one's life and actions from the inside outwards. This is striking, given the context of existing tradition and people's expectations in that time of foreign domination and oppression. The focus of Jesus, as of those who went before him, is certainly on the coming Reign of God, and on what must be done to welcome it into human society. What is new and particular in his message is the urgency and the proclamation of human empowerment. The Reign of God is not to be thought of as an arbitrary gift of God, unrelated to human behavior, readiness, and response. The Reign of God, according to the teaching of Jesus, is among the people, within them, and at hand. But it is a gift that can be received only by means of a very radical turnabout in the way individuals and societies usually behave.

The Reign of God is the reign of true peace among human beings in all their affairs. On this Jesus was in agreement with his critics and his enemies. But he astonished his friends and provoked his enemies by his perception of the means to that condition of true peace. Neither seizure of political power whether by violence or by any kind of clever maneuver, nor skilful compromise and arrangement with the occupation forces, nor yet reliance upon religious ritual or upon withdrawal from public affairs as much as possible was either acceptable as a means or relevant to true peace according to the divine rule as Jesus saw it and proposed it to his followers. Jesus taught his followers a way of life that envisaged the rebuilding of society as genuine and non-inclusive community from the grass roots up. Such community building is also necessarily from the inside of the individual outwards. Most striking of his teachings are the apparently impossible sayings of the Sermon on the Mount, giving a glimpse of the drastic kind of response that will truly make the reign of the God of peace a reality in the world and its history. The Beatitudes as listed in chapter 5 of Matthew's Gospel link the attainment of the divine reign of peace and well-being directly with humility, gentleness, willingness to suffer in the cause of right, wholehearted pursuit of what is right, mercy and compassion, purity or simplicity of heart, and an attitude of peaceableness. Moreover, the passages immediately following propose a level of selflessness that would usually be regarded as heroic in the world. To this is added an insistence on the essential interiority of the Law that constitutes Israel's convenant with God. Honesty, truth, non-violence, chastity, and justice are to be found in people's hearts and intentions before they are expressed in actions. The essence of worship is not in the words recited or in ritual performances but in the inner disposition of mind and heart. When people have their attention fixed on the Reign of God in trust and simplicity, they will not be wearied and oppressed by anxieties concerning their livelihood and security.

Peaceable Means to the Reign of God

Christians are accustomed to read these texts as a guide to the way they should ideally be living. But it is important to note that the teaching of Jesus is not moralistic but revelatory. Jesus, like the Buddha, shows his followers truths they must recognize for themselves in their own experience and reflection before these truths can have real meaning for them. What Jesus is saying in the Sermon on the Mount is not simply that people ought to behave the way he is describing, nor even that they must behave this way in order to earn a reward, but rather that this is the very nature of the Reign of God with its content of peace and human happiness. The goal is like this and the only possible means to the goal are those that participate in the nature and character of the goal. The Reign of peace is reached by peaceable means. However, peaceable means do not consist of doing nothing; they consist of a deep transformation of society that begins with self-transformation of individuals, which in turn begins with the transformation of interior attitudes, values, and expectations.

The Price of Peace and the World Religions

In all of this Buddhism and Christianity are much alike. However, one strong difference arises in relation to the price to be paid for peace, harmony, and happiness in life. The Middle Way of Buddhism, while requiring discipline and renunciation, does not focus on self-sacrifice, perhaps because of the teaching that the self is not a permanent entity. Christianity from the outset has focused on the goal of happiness in the Reign of God but emphasized very strongly that there is a price to be paid in suffering for the restored harmony, simply because everything in human affairs has become so distorted through sin. In the earliest centuries of the Church that was so much part of the Christian outlook that martyrdom was greatly revered as an intimate partnership with Jesus in the nonviolent testimony that would turn the world back to God as its source, its harmony, and its end. Christian faith was able to provide the motivation for large numbers of very ordinary people to take such an heroic stance.

Where Buddhism and Christianity have been concerned with the virtues and attitudes that lead to a peaceable life and therefore a genuinely peaceable society, focusing on the personal transformation, Judaism and Islam have addressed the structure of society directly by their focus on the Law as revealed by God to shape the People of God. For both Judaism and Islam, the word for peace, *shalom, salaam,* is used as a greeting because it contains the fulness of what is good that can be wished to anyone. As mentioned in chapter 4, the notion of *shalom* carries the content certainly of freedom from war and violence, but also freedom from anxiety and threats, and the positive content of well-being, of modest sufficiency, support of friends and family, and so forth. This more comprehensive peace is the gift of God to those who submit themselves to God by living according to the Law of God as it has been shown to them through prophets and tradition. In the Judaic way of looking at the human situation, a covenant with God is very important. The life of human society in God's world can fit together smoothly and harmoniously, but on God's terms, and these have to be studied because the consequences of evil deeds have distorted so much of our perception and our customs. Moreover, the Law which God reveals not only has to be studied, but it must be implemented in every detail and aspect of life. This requires a good deal of self-discipline from all the participants, a self-discipline learned by conscientious observation of a prescribed code for behavior and relationships. However, this is not to be regarded as a burden but as a great privilege—the privilege of sharing in God's own wisdom and in an intimate alliance with God.[26]

In Islam, submission to Allah, the Lord of the Worlds, involves all the structures of society and is the means for transforming fear into peace. This understanding that submission to God is not only a private matter for individuals but a matter for society has led to the four great traditions of Islamic Law in which the actual implementation of a just and peaceful society is spelled out. The social teachings of Islam are explicit and detailed, encompassing economic justice and compassion, placing great emphasis on racial justice, and among other aspects going into detail about ways to deal with conflict by arbitration and negotiation to avoid war and other kinds of violence.[27]

This emphasis on the social structure and conduct of society can easily be misrepresented and misunderstood. It is an expression of the conviction that people's personal lives and attitudes are shaped by their experiences in society and that the structures, laws, and relationships set up in society largely determine what the experiences of people living in that society will be. Thus it places emphasis on the influence that flows from outside inwards, where Buddhism and Christianity tend to place more emphasis on the influence that flows from inside outward. But it should be evident to a careful observer that actually all these traditions are concerned with the inseparable unity of personal and social dimensions of life.

Moreover, they all in fact contain teachings for the individual and teachings for the society, and they all value the interrelationship between inner and outer peace and the price of peace which is a discipline that links the inner and outer aspects.

Though it is certainly not a religion, it may be worth noting that Marxism is a tradition whose teachings emphasize very strongly the influence that moves from outside in. The restructuring of social forces will, according to the writings of Karl Marx himself, eventually produce the new human being who will think more in terms of "ours" than "mine," and who will not seek personal satisfaction in hoarding wealth or in dominating and surpassing others in various ways. These were going to be new human beings, essentially in their peaceableness and creative energies poured into collaboration in a profound sense of attaining their true being as human persons.

The kind of transformations of society that Marx envisaged have never been systematically tried, though they have been implemented somewhat more in west European social democracies than in the communist countries, notwithstanding the fact that it is the latter who claimed Marxism as their basic philosophy and platform. As a peacemaking philosophy, Marxism is certainly not wholly wrong, because it emphasizes the destructive power of greed and accumulation and the way these tend to be reflected at the political and cultural level (including the religious). In this it is at one with the teachings of the great religions about the price of peace which includes detachment from greed for possessions. Moreover, the Marxist analysis of the woes of society teaches the ordinary working people and the poor who generally bear the brunt of war that they cannot gain anything by fighting those who are just like themselves but under the power of a different set of rulers and employers. Peace is, therefore, an integral part of the Marxist hope and promise. But because of the extreme reluctance of Marx himself to admit ethical categories or spiritual realities, there is a certain lack of motivation in doing all that is really necessary for peacemaking.

While traditions mentioned so far emphasize either the personal or the social dimension but include both, the traditions of China rather explicitly acknowledge the balance by the way in which the teachings of Confucius on social proprieties and proper relations are combined with the teachings of Taoism on *wu wei*, a mental and personal inner peacefulness and harmony with the greater reality of the world and its rhythms, offering spontaneity, simplicity, and adaptability. The Tao, or "way," is at the same time the hidden inner mystery of all reality, and the way of the universe or nature, and within that the way which is the appropriate or truly human way to live. The way, therefore, requires the overcoming of prejudices, false expectations, and so forth, and is seen as one aspect of the price of peace, just as the Confucian teachings point to another and complementary aspect of the price of peace.[28]

The foregoing has by no means exhausted the number of the world's religions, much less has it given the teachings of any one tradition in any depth. It will have been enough to demonstrate that the religious outlook on life, which in much of the world is not strictly separated from the political and economic affairs of whole countries or from their foreign policies, offers foundations and motivations which go beyond the more usual rational approach to diplomacy and foreign affairs. It is a characteristic prejudice of the post-Enlightenment western industrialized countries that isolates the conduct of public policy from the more fundamental convictions which people hold about the nature and meaning of the reality in which they live. While this offers the possibility of a broader range of shared public discourse, it may fall short of the motivations which really affect people, and it may fail to enlist sufficient motivation to pay the price of a genuine peace.

7

Peacefulness, a Personal Discipline

From the discussion in the foregoing chapters, several matters should have become plain and several issues should have come into focus. From reflection on what wars do and do not bring about in human society and in the ecology and economy, the voice of reason concludes that wars are not the answer to the desires for which they are usually fought. From the testimonies of the religious traditions of the human race, it is clear that a hope for peace which is informed by faith is very widely shared among the peoples of the earth. A review of discussions and arguments based only in reason and observation shows that the notion of a thorough and permanent world peace is not absurd but in keeping with the nature of human beings and with their situation in the world and its history.

Motivation toward Peace

The question as to why, then, peace is not universally achieved leads to the claim of several of the great religious traditions of the world that peace is a divine gift to be received upon terms divinely established. The question whether in that case people can do anything about it is clearly answered from practice and from theory: peace has its logic and can be pursued in a reasonable quest not difficult to discover or understand. Further, the reiterated question as to why it does not happen if peacemaking is not difficult to understand leads to the crux of the matter which is not in understanding but in willing; the religions of the world offer the testimony that peace has its price, and that this price requires powerful motivation because it requires radical conversion of mentality, activity, and relationships. What is particularly encouraging, however, is that peace is such a pervasive theme in the major religious traditions and that this offers such extensive common ground for the building of common expectations and understandings.

One of the more important points of common agreement among the religious traditions, which form such a large component of the heritage of human wisdom, is the insistence that peacemaking does not begin, or even have its most important moment, at the conference tables where representatives of various nations gather. Prior to the encounter of nations with one another is the building of nations which are peaceful within their own borders. This involves a just and responsible economy—just in that it embraces all in its opportunities for production and consumption according to their talents and their needs, and responsible in that it is adapted to meet real human needs, not artificially generated needs, much less means of mass destruction. Such an economy, in turn, does not happen except in a culture that values those things that build community, foster long-term hope, respect every person, treasure truth and honesty, inculcate courtesy and compassion, emphasize the beautiful and harmonious, and do not allow leisure to be eliminated from people's lives for material gain.

The making, adapting, and sustaining of the culture is in the hands of all the people, and here particularly the individual as individual can make a difference. Not surprisingly, all the religious traditions when addressing the question of peace teach a personal spirituality of peace for the individual. The twentieth century has been rich with movements which have banded people together voluntarily in a quest for peaceable life-styles and peacemaking patterns of association, action, and even protest. At the end of this century, one does not have to begin from nothing in such a quest but can come into the inheritance of a rich cross-fertilization of the traditions. Without attempting to credit each idea or aspect precisely to one or another tradition, therefore, this chapter will attempt to set forth some well-tested wisdom for peaceable living.

Wisdom for Peaceable Living

According to the cumulative wisdom to be garnered from the age-old traditions, a personal discipline of peacefulness begins with a rhythm of life in which there are periods of silence, of quieting of desires and preoccupations, of contemplation and meditation, of prayer. All traditions point to the need to pause for focus and perspective, to consider the hierarchy of one's values, to compare explicitly claimed values with practically operative (and perhaps unnoticed or unrecognized) values. But the occasions for acquiring such focus and perspective are not identical with what in our western culture we usually regard as recreation. Entertainment by sound waves or screen may afford a certain kind of relaxation from worry and stressful preoccupations, which is helpful in enabling people to continue with their work or social responsibilities without breaking down or burning out. But this is not a help in bringing a surer, truer focus to one's life and thought because the psychological distance it gives leaves a cluttered and not an empty space. Psychological distance from work, possessions, daily affairs, and obligations and preoccupations is necessary, but if it is to give not only temporary relief from pressure but also a certain freedom to evaluate, to reconsider, and to change in fundamental ways, the space created needs to be a space empty of clutter. All the religious traditions teach ways of prayer which lead to meditation (quiet, peaceful reflection on fundamental truths which shape human life and awareness) and to contemplation (receptive presence).

Sometimes people testify that illness, tragedy, or the death of close friends or relatives have influenced them to reexamine their own values, or perhaps have spontaneously regrouped or reorganized what they saw as of greatest importance. Simple human realities of life itself, family bonds, community support, come to supplant ambitions and possessions as the central values, and these simple realities are those which are most likely to provide motivation for common endeavor and least likely to promote cut-throat competition. But the unanimous teaching of the religious traditions is that it is not necessary to wait for death or tragedy to intervene. We shape our own lives to a very large extent by the decisions we make personally, and together we shape our society by those decisions. To appropriate our freedom to shape our lives in depth and fulness, one of the first requirements is simply to become aware of the direction and thrust of our own habitual choices and expectations and to question them in a context of quiet detachment. A life that contains a rhythm of such quiet times makes this possible, and most traditions have emphasized that it needs to be a daily rhythm to be truly effective.

Reflection Helps Resolve Inner Conflicts

Clearly, one of the fruits of outer silence and inner quiet is that issues which are usually pushed outside the scope of attention have an opportunity to come to the surface. For instance, most people have inner conflicts, which because they have not been resolved have been projected onto other people or groups creating hostilities. In American culture one of the most troublesome of such inner conflicts is the unacknowledged conflict of two commonly accepted values: to be nice to everyone and to compete as hard as possible for status, income, power, privileges, and so forth. It is not possible to do both of these things wholeheartedly, though one might alternate, or do one in some situations and the other in other situations. There is a great deal in the nurture of Americans and in public rhetoric and advertising that presents both these ideals as comprehensive without ever acknowledging the need for sacrifices and choices. In a frantically busy and more or less unexamined life, the conflict can be acute but unrecognized. It readily becomes projected into such perceptions as the following: it is the wife and children who are holding the husband and father back from the promotion he should have achieved long ago; it is the immigrants who are interfering with the labor market and causing the trouble; it is the prejudice of employers or supervisors that makes the situation tense and unsatisfying; it is the racial minorities demanding equality that have deprived the dominant group of their rights, and so forth. Another form of the same inner conflict is the idea, much inculcated by educational and other patterns of competition, that to be happy and fulfilled in life, to be a "success" one must be the top, the first, "number one." Again, in an unexamined life it leads to much grief, sense of total failure, anger against those seen as responsible for the defeat, and so forth.

Quiet reflection, times of silence and of contemplative posture, allow the inner conflicts to rise to the surface and reveal themselves as such, sloughing off the disguise that presents them as other people's hostility or malfeasance. Such times therefore allow for a clarification of values and goals and an emergence of a more authentically human set of expectations and assessments. Quiet reflection shows that it is not necessary to be "number one" to be happy; it is not necessary to see everything in life as a competition; in a competition not everyone can win, but in cooperation the gain of each is the gain of all; having friendly relations with all places restraints both on the desirability and on the need of competition. It should be evident that the paradigms for our relationships with one another as individuals, as families, professional or interest groups, and so forth become also the paradigms for our national relationships with other nations, and the inner contradictions are easily projected onto the other nations as unfair competitors or hostile forces. The larger the arena, the greater the violence that may result, but the principles are fundamentally the same at all levels of social organization and can be corrected by working from the simplest level upwards to the most complex.

Reordering of the Hierarchy of Values

Becoming aware of inner conflicts and of false or distorted or inflated desires which cannot bring fulfillment is a necessary beginning, but it must lead not to discouragement or cynicism but to change. Clarification of values and goals is helpful, but it should lead to a reordering of the hierarchy of values. This is an area in which all the major religious traditions of the world have perfected insight and teaching over many centuries, whether it be by the guidance in creative quietude in Taoism, by stories from the Upanishads, by the precepts of the Eightfold Path, by the striving which is the true Jihad, by the precepts of the Sinai covenant, or by the teachings derived from the Gospels. What the religions have to offer is a teaching based on promises of true happiness already demonstrated by the heroes and saints of each tradition, as well as the support of a community of shared vision, experience, and life to make the reordering of values and expectations realistically possible. Within each community of faithful followers this offers some precedents which justify further expectations, and what is exemplified within the communities is shown in principle to be possible also among them. Moreover, closer study shows the high degree of congruence among the various traditions in their guidance concerning which are good and appropriate desires and in what forms or under what conditions human desires become riotous and destructive.

Developing Compassion

One particular aspect of this common teaching which should perhaps be especially noted is the need to develop the fullest possible compassion. Compassion is based in empathy but it is more than empathy. Empathy, the capacity to know and imagine what the other is feeling, is a very basic ingredient of being human. If offers bridges of access into other people's experience. But empathy is also practiced by the salesperson and the advertiser, usually for motives of commercial profit. Empathy is practiced to a high degree by the torturer whose success depends on accurately imagining the victim's physical pain, emotional feelings, thoughts and attitudes, so as to know how to break that person's resistance. We shudder at the mention of torture, yet in subtle forms much torture, especially of a psychological kind, is practiced in our society, and it depends on a certain cultivation of empathy. It is true that it is an inferior and inadequate empathy because it only develops power to destroy, not to build up. Even in the work of destruction it is often shortsighted, not looking beyond the immediate goal of surrender to see the forces of vindication and of raw revenge building up for the future.

Sympathy or compassion, however, is not only a matter of insight into the experience of the other but of entering into it with one's own feelings and vulnerability to share the experience. The development of true compassion means that I am truly and painfully oppressed when the other is oppressed, terrified in the fear of the other, crushed and depressed in the sufferings of the other, and seeking my own liberation in the liberation of the other. Hence true compassion is the very substance of peace and the central path of peacemaking. It is the kind of force which arises spontaneously in parents, perhaps especially in mothers, in relation to their children, at least while they are young. The child is experienced as almost one in being with the parent, who is in distress when the child cries, serene in the child's contentment, and proud of the child's achievements as though these were the parent's. The parent does not feel rejected by the child's increasing independence but experiences this as shared freedom. In fact, when the small child, irritable with fatigue, fever, teething, or something else, lashes out against the parent, the parent is likely to feel the distress of the child rather than any resentment against the child for the hostility expressed. This is described in the forgiveness of Jesus on the cross and in the last words of many martyrs. It is a transcending of the isolation of individual human experience in the maturity of personhood and in the strength of community bonds. Out of this kind of compassion, intensively developed by many people, great violence and enmity can be overcome. Gandhi's *swaraj* movement, Martin Luther King's civil rights movement, Danilo Dolci's work in Sicily, and the non-violent revolution in the Philippines stand as monuments to the power of such levels of transcending compassion.

Cultivating Authentic Dialogue

One principal way of cultivating the virtue of compassion is by the practice of authentic dialogue at every level of human relationships and social structures. A genuine dialogue is marked by open hospitality with one's own ideas, experiences, and perspectives and by friendly curiosity about those of the others. Dialogue differs from argument, though the latter is sometimes useful as in the trying of a case in court or the consideration of the advisability of a piece of legislation. In such arguments each side puts its own case as forcefully as possible with the hope of persuading a third party who must decide between them. Even in an argument, if it is honestly and well conducted, there is often a resolution which is not identical with the position proposed initially by either side, but which is a compromise or new proposal transcending both. In a dialogue, however, this is foreseen at the outset and desired. Each gives at least as much energy and attention to listening as to speaking. The aim is to learn as much as possible from the other and to offer one's own insights, beliefs, and so forth as a gift to the other that may enrich and broaden the view from the other side. The effort in dialogue is to enhance one's own experience by attempts to see situations and possibilities from another's point of view.

All collaboration and all social life depends heavily upon such dialogue, but there are factors in modern technological societies that preempt dialogue and isolate people from one another. The larger and more complex society is, the more social and economic intercourse must be regulated by official and impersonal controls. But the more such controls are operative in the society, the more people function according to the laws and regulations and not according to relationships with other persons. There is a general depersonalizing effect on relationships in which other people come to be seen and experienced as functions, services, part of the machinery rather than persons. Where this happens, less and less true dialogue goes on, people are emotionally and intellectually isolated, and their capacity for compassion shrinks, eventually stunting even the basic human faculty of empathy. Some such effect has often been highly visible in international relations. For instance, in the "Cold War" period the United States administration consistently assumed that an overwhelming buildup of kill-power on the American side would keep the Soviet sector peaceful—a staggering failure to exercise enough empathy even to ask what the American response was to any buildup of Soviet kill-power, namely, a sense of danger, of imminent crisis, of desirability of preemptive strikes, and so forth. To calm observers, it was quite extraordinary that "national defense" could be based on such inability to calculate the reactions on the other side. The same may be said of the many wars of intervention and manipulation of small nations during the time of the Communiphobia—never the realization that American threats or attacks would naturally prompt small nations to look to alliance with the other great power of the world, whereas friendly overtures would at the least allow them the freedom to choose.

Freire and Critical Consciousness

The exercise of dialogue at all levels of relationship, besides being personally enriching and boosting personal security and therefore supporting personal peacefulness directly, contributes to the development of "critical consciousness" in the sense in which that term is used in the theory of Paolo Freire.[29] Critical consciousness in this sense is an important tool for peace. It is the mature stage of human consciousness, though it is not reached without considerable effort and training.

According to Freire's insightful theory, human consciousness begins in an "immersed" condition, that is, it simply records what is going on uncritically, regarding things in nature and affairs in human society as simply given, inevitable, in an undifferentiated way. This is proper to the child who must first find out what is going on in the world before assuming any responsibilities within it or making any critical judgments about it. It is not, however, appropriate for a human being to remain indefinitely in this state of passive acceptance of all that is. It is appropriate, and in most cases happens, that the individual begins to develop semi-critical and naively critical areas of consciousness. In this phase, semi-critical consciousness takes stock of some situations and assumes some responsibility for the way things are, perhaps in family life, in small voluntary associations, in a craft or business, and in many choices in private life. However, it is a semi-critical consciousness because it is inadvertently selective, recognizing human responsibility in some aspects of life but seeing many other affairs as inevitable which are in reality humanly constituted and call for the assumption of personal responsibility. It is in this way that public affairs, even in highly literate democratic countries, often get out of control because people do not think they have the power to control them. It is in this way that a desire for peace which is strong and pervasive throughout a whole population may nevertheless be ineffective in influencing national policy.

Particularly important from the point of view of peacemaking is the other aspect which Freire's theory points to in the development of critical consciousness. There is an inevitable stage of growth, and it may be a very long one, when consciousness is not only semi-critical in the way just explained, but is also naively critical. One aspect of this naïveté is the tendency to look for and try to eliminate the "guilty party" in any situation causing suffering, oppression, or violence, rather than trying to understand what it is in the system, the structure, the values, and expectations of all participants that operates to oppress or hurt in various ways. As history has long shown, the elimination of tyrants by violence seldom resolves the problem because it sets up a new kind of violence in order to defend and maintain what has been gained by the violent overthrow of the tyrant. But this type of response is just one example of a broader range of naïveté—the tendency to look for the simple, quick solution, to want a problem solved without a great deal of effort, to see everything in terms of clear black and white distinctions, to suppose that what has gone wrong has done so because those in charge were evil and could foresee all the consequences from the beginning. To overcome this kind of impatience and false simplification of everything that demands human responsibility and participation is very important for peacemaking, and the transcending of this phase of human consciousness is what is meant by critical consciousness.

Critical consciousness requires a good deal of self-knowledge (to recognize one's own prejudices) and self-discipline (to take the time and make the effort required even to understand situations correctly) as well as a high degree of collaboration (to share and exchange the various types of expertise often required, to build the persuasive power of numbers, and to find the social pressure points at which a difference can be made). To build this kind of consciousness should be the aim of all education, but as Freire himself has often pointed out, education is more often deflected from its proper human purpose and used to blunt critical consciousness with ideological indoctrination, that is, with normative theories which obscure or suppress the facts and the desire to ask questions about the facts. Unfortunately this often happens quite early in the lives of young people, before they have progressed far in naïve and semiconsciousness. It is one of the major forces working against peace because it is a force that builds prejudices and unreflective loyalties. It is a force which equates patriotism with the kind of nationalism that proclaims loyalty to one's own country, whether right or wrong. However, the loyalty is not usually expressed in this way; the question whether the decisions of one's own government and its policies are right or wrong is simply not raised on the understanding that this would be disloyal, unpatriotic. That this is not even in accord with the principles of democracy is often glossed over.

With such educational obstruction of the development of critical consciousness, social injustices and oppressions are not readily recognized, and the justification for the country's declaration of war does not come under scrutiny. This is not simply because people are unwilling to assess events and situations critically, but because it does not occur to them to do so because they do not really see an injustice or oppression. What they see is the government, which is always right, minding its public business while private citizens should mind their own private business. Clearly, there is always a crack through which new light may come at times of election and at times when the country is shaken by some scandal in government or some utterly unexpected event in world affairs, but the trend is dangerous, and the way to peace and justice requires the development towards critical consciousness of as many people as possible.

While Freire's terminology is new, the basic insights are not. He has given explicit articulation to something that is implicit in the religious traditions. The prophetic and spiritual strands in the great religious traditions have been countercultural in their drawing out of a consciousness critical of the prevailing assumptions and values of their societies, although it is true that the institutional elements in all the major traditions have practiced ideological indoctrination like all other institutional structures. But the religions have lived and survived and revived as a powerful force in the world because of the perennial freshness of the spirituality and the prophetic elements, not because of the solidity of the institutional structures. Those spirituality traditions have taught basic personal virtues and attitudes which have offered foundations and bonds for peaceable human societies. Some of these virtues are not spectacular but make a crucial difference in the quality of life for all. For instance, the religious traditions commonly call for courtesy and friendliness in all dealings with other people. Courtesy may seem like a small matter in human relationships, but it makes many relationships possible which otherwise would not occur at all, and it depends on a high degree of personal development, including patience, self-control, attention, sensitive empathy, respect for tradition, and so forth. Similarly, friendliness of manner invites trust, builds community bonds, promotes true dialogue and peaceful relations, but depends on self-possession, fearlessness, generosity, attentiveness, and self-control.

Building Blocks for a Peaceable Society

The spirituality traditions of the great religions have also emphasized some indispensable building blocks for a peaceable society such as respect for the lives, well-being, safety, property, and reputation of all. These are not exclusively religious demands or attitudes; civil society guarantees them to some minimal degree by external sanctions in the form of threats of penalties. What the religious traditions add to this is a certain enhancement and refinement in degree of sensitivity and response based on the anthropology taught by the religions and relating everyday encounters in society to the ultimate meaning and purpose of human life.

The difference between minimal guaranteed respect for human life and the fullest sensitivity to the worth of other persons is a very great difference and affects the quality of life as well as the chances of survival. It will, for instance, affect the infant mortality rate among the poor by determining how comprehensive proper health care is for those who cannot pay private insurance. It will influence whether poor people spend their lives in beautiful or squalid surroundings, and whether young people of minority groups have the motivation to remain in school and qualify to earn their living with dignity and pride. Minimal protection of life by law often punishes the taking of life by street violence but ignores the loss or diminution of life by systemic violence from which so many people of the world suffer generation after generation. Respect for life and all the goods that go with it really requires positive and creative action for the building and betterment of society as well as emergency preventive measures. But civic laws cannot require such creative positive action; the motivation and the guidance for this must come from the private initiative of the citizens, and their best source of inspiration is in the religious traditions.

Concern Always for the Poorest

From the prophetic strands of the religious traditions comes an even more powerful inspiration for the personal discipline of peacefulness, and that is the imperative to look out always for the poorest, the most marginated and neglected, the least regarded or respected. The logic of this bias is, of course, that it is corrective. It leans towards those least able to speak for themselves and be heard, those least able to claim their rights, whose needs are also the most urgent. That there should be such a bias toward the poorest is easy to understand in theory but very seldom observed in practice. More commonly people feel they have earned the advantages they have in life, and that it is right that they should be rewarded even if others are left out. The personal practice of looking out for the poorest does not come to people spontaneously but must be cultivated deliberately. When it is practiced extensively in any local community, it makes for peace because the needs of all are met, and there is much less fear of losing possessions through robbery or theft, less fear for one's personal safety from violence or the disruption of life in the community. The same principle applies in the international community. If the needs of the poorest populations are met, there is a general reduction of refugee populations and problems; there is less fear of grave epidemics spreading through other areas carried by travelers from the neglected areas; there is less incentive for terrorist attacks by frustrated and desperate people, and so forth.

Distinction Between Responsibility and Guilt

Finally, critical to the personal discipline of peacefulness and peacemaking is the distinction between responsibility and guilt. People often react with anger to suggestions that they should accept social responsibility because they confuse this with being accused of guilt in the bringing about of the problem or need in the first place. Most large problems of society have grown over long periods of time or have a long pre-history. Those presently alive have often been born into a situation which is therefore not of their making. It is even possible that the whole situation came about through inadvertence or through circumstances beyond human control altogether, so that no one is to blame. But we are the co-creators of the world and society of our own time and of the future. We carry responsibility for what we make of those things that are now within our power. Guilt looks to the past, but responsibility looks to the future. A personal discipline of peacefulness and peacemaking necessarily involves the acceptance of social responsibility. This is a responsibility that cannot be prescribed in its concrete detail because it depends on creativity, initiative, seizing the moment, taking risks.

8

A Peaceable Future: The Nurturing Task

A peaceable way of life is certainly something that can be taught. Some societies have done it much better than others. Some ways of nurturing and socializing the young are more peace directed than others. As a general principle it is safe to say that people become more irritable, restless, and quarrelsome in proportion as they experience frustration, and that they are likely to be more peaceful, friendly, and helpful when they experience acceptance, achievement, and satisfaction of basic needs. We have become used to this idea in relation to juvenile delinquents, especially those who come from situations of extreme deprivation, but we certainly need to extend this to the consideration of the entire environment which nurtures the young of our society. That includes, of course, the family and the school, but it also applies to sports and entertainment, to what they see in advertising, in the role models who are prominently featured in press and media, and to many other aspects of our society which are in fact formative influences though they may not be so intended.

Nurturing by Families

Unfortunately, parents do not have as much influence in their children's lives as they formerly did. It is true that a family life which meets basic human needs and inspires modest and attainable desires in the way of material possessions and practical opportunities offers a far more secure beginning than one which does not do this. It is also true that parents who are themselves disciplined, peaceful, generous and just, and compassionate and sensitive to others' needs will be powerfully influential role models. But parents can no longer protect their children from exposure to destructive forces in society—the promotion of false values and disordered desires, the evoking of unquenchable cupidity, and shame, anger and envy over what others have more than themselves, the expectation that the least desire ought to be gratified instantly, and the sense that all goals should be attainable without hard, boring, or uncongenial work. Parents cannot protect their children from exposure to this kind of propaganda, whether blatant or subtle.

In a capitalist society the media are for the most part run for profit, and are largely financed by advertising. As Marx pointed out long ago, companies try to expand their profits and markets, striving to survive over against their competitors, and they subordinate the welfare not only of their workers (which is something that modern nations have controlled with legislation) but also of those who constitute their market. With the increase of production the companies try to expand their markets by stimulating more felt needs, which soon become artificial needs. They target the audience or readership which is easiest to influence, and that is mainly children and adolescents. The programs directed to them are often not conceived in their interest but in that of the advertiser. The means by which they are influenced are, of course, the arousing of discontent (of all kinds of artificial hungers which are never satisfied by the objects proposed) and envy (the persistent message that other people all have these things and are made blissfully happy by them).

Families cannot protect their children from exposure to this kind of corruption, but for any kind of balance and serenity they must try to counteract the influence by the example of a happy life with modest possessions and opportunities and reasonable components of hard work and delayed satisfaction of needs and desires. Discussion of the problem helps but does not solve it. Early association with likeminded families can be a great support if such families can be found through religious, professional, neighborhood, or other contacts, but many parents find it extremely discouraging to try to find other parents who share countercultural values of this kind and are also geographically near enough and free at the right times for a sustained association. It would be a helpful pattern for schools and churches to foster.

Nurturing by Schools

Beyond what families themselves can do, young people's experience and expectations and values are shaped very much by the schools, not only by what is explicitly in the curriculum but by what they pick up from the way things are done. From the point of view of the fostering of peaceable persons, perhaps the first aspect to be noted is the extent to which most schools are based on competition rather than cooperation. This may be stimulating and exciting for those with superior talent and home background, but it is stiflingly frustrating for those whose natural abilities are notably less or are in fields not rewarded in a school education.

The greater the emphasis on competition, the larger the proportionate number of those who will feel frustrated by failure and lack of recognition and appreciation. Such frustration will result in the irritable restlessness and anger which is the very opposite of peaceable personality. What exacerbates the effect of the general competitive spirit of academic life in schools is the fact that at least in the public school system of America sports have also become not a relaxing physical activity for all, but a selective process focused on interscholastic competitive teams in which very, very few can play, though all are given the sense that they must reach one of these teams to be successful. The schools are full of athletic young people who know they are good players but were not chosen and feel very bitter and cheated. If less emphasis were placed on the selection and promotion of the very few, many could find a deeply satisfying outlet in playing the sport for sport.

Peace Education

Peace education has to be a style of education which encourages the development of talents and skills without linking success to the failure of someone else. This requires some thought and planning but it can be done. It can be done in various ways by appreciating or rewarding of class projects in which all participate, by extending sports activities to many intramural teams and games while de-emphasizing the interscholastic, and perhaps most of all by present-ing the preparation for different types of work for a livelihood as worthwhile options in the course of schooling.

It has been amply demonstrated that the present public school system of the United States is geared to those with primarily aca-demic and traditional professional inclinations, which includes only 5 or 6 percent of the population. Teaching styles have been found to be directed to this small segment with its characteristic ways of assimilating knowledge. The large numbers of young people who learn better by doing and who would profit by apprenticeship train-ing in practical matters at an early age are subjected to unnecessary levels of frustration throughout their school years, and among minority and poor students many are branded as "high school drop-outs," somehow indicating that they have already failed as human beings. While it is clearly no contribution to a peaceful society to have young people roam city streets unemployed, the constant negative stress of a high school curriculum that does not meet their needs or develop their best talents may not be a great deal better. Many European countries have found ways to offer a more varied range of educational options, maintaining the dignity and self-respect of people in crafts and practical skills.

Those young people whom we now send to colleges and univer-sities may also give some pause for thought about the relationship between the development of a peaceable personality and the way the educational process is experienced. The heavy emphasis on grades, down to decimal points of distinction, the frequency of test-ing and recording of scores, the competition for placement at the more prestigious (not necessarily better) colleges and graduate schools, are all factors that tend to detract from the intrinsic in-terest of the subject matter studied. Moreover, they are factors which tend to concentrate the attention of the students on them-selves as individuals rather than on their own interaction within community structures. As is well known, the worst example of this is in the processes throughout college years that contribute to the selection for medical schools, and which are not constituted to give us the most generous and compassionate medical doctors for the future. Although some colleges, especially church related ones, do offer students the opportunity and invitation to be active in voluntary work for the needy, higher education in general in the American context does not favor the development of compassion and public concern.

Some of the factors that can be developed in the direction of peace education are already in place, at least in some institutions. Most obviously, many colleges and a few high schools have international exchange programs for summers or for whole scholastic years for a limited number of qualifying students. One could hope to see this developed. Prejudice feeds on ignorance, and prejudice makes misunderstandings, failures of empathy, and groundless hostilities very likely in human situations. The remedy for prejudice is to come to know some of the "other side" personally, share activities, learn the language, talk together, get to know one another well. The international exchange programs run by schools are a helpful beginning towards this, and might encourage personal initiatives to continue or extend the experience and to draw others into it.

Peace Education and Liberal Studies

What may be less obvious is the relation of genuinely liberal studies to peace education. Unfortunately, much current higher education in the United States is quite technical, specialized, in the area of acquiring skills. It prepares people to function in the expected way in a predetermined slot in a company, organization, or system, to adopt the outlook, values, and expectations of the system, and to ask those questions, and only those questions, which get the job done efficiently. The problem with this type of education is that it does not prompt people to ask more basic questions about the system itself, its underlying values, its impact on human beings, especially on those who may be considered outsiders or less important to the system.

This is the function of a true liberal arts education: to prompt critical reflection on values and assumptions of one's own society, to look at the historical development of various aspects of civilization and to consider alternative developments, those that might have been and those that were in fact pursued by other societies.

A liberal education prompts people to ask ethical questions, philosophical questions, aesthetic questions. In other words, it is a means of shaping citizens who recognize and accept their own role in the shaping of their culture, their economy, their country's international relations, and so forth. In our society, with its heavy emphasis on profit and efficiency, there is a tendency for liberal arts colleges to be drawn closer and closer to technical schools so as to enable students to compete more effectively in the job market immediately upon graduation. It is a move in the direction of peacemaking and peace education for the future to strive against this trend and to maintain genuine liberal arts colleges with genuinely liberal curricula.

It is, however, not only families and schools which nurture the future and have an impact on its character, whether peaceable or otherwise. The media, both informational and entertaining, shape the thinking and attitudes of young people without the latter's being aware of it and shape their thinking often to be quite prejudiced, and to value material possessions, appearance, style more than substance and character. As already mentioned, this is not likely to change in commercial television in a capitalist society because the programs will be used to sell something, and companies will try to find something to sell that people do not already have, which in an affluent culture is likely to be something they do not need and which does not really provide more happiness or fulfillment. Because the commercial media are always going to be at the mercy of this pattern of causality, it might be noted that a significant input into peace education in the broad sense can be through public television and radio programs. Support for them financially, as well as recording requests and evaluations, is a worthwhile contribution to channels of information and entertainment which are less vulnerable to the distortion endemic to commercial media.

Nurturing by Churches and Religious Groups

Finally, Churches and religious groups of all faiths and all types play a central role in the personal formation of those whom they reach. As shown in chapters 2, 4, and 6, all the faith traditions have strong components of peace teachings, spiritualities of non-violence, classic texts considering peaceful alternatives to wars among peoples, and so forth. What is not so evident is that these are communicated in the ordinary process of the handing on of the heritage from generation to generation or from the old established groups to the newcomers of each age. It seems that more often the emphasis in religious instruction is on ritual elements which distinguish each group from other faiths or other denominations, accompanied by some rules for personal behavior in specific commandments and prohibitions. But this is not adequate for a teaching of peaceable and non-violent ways. The sorrows and sufferings of societies as they in fact exist in the world will not be overcome by the observance of specific commands and prohibitions but only by a creative, compassionate response that goes far beyond anything that can be specifically commanded. The role of churches and religious bodies in passing on a spirituality of non-violence and peacemaking is a critical and central one which these bodies cannot afford to neglect.

9

A Peaceable Nation: Social and Political Action

Many readers may be inclined to skip this chapter on the assumption that social and political action is open only to people with special training and opportunities. But this quite contradicts all the principles on which democratic societies are built. Social and political action is the privilege and duty of everyone, and it has a great variety of forms. It ranges from voting in elections to acts of civil disobedience, from running for office and serving on legislative bodies to lobbying, from becoming well informed on national and international issues to getting something done about local traffic lights and potholes in the streets. Most of us are so preoccupied with our families, jobs, housekeeping, and face-to-face contacts that it is very easy to fall into Freire's category of semi-critical consciousness; we tend to focus our responsibility and awareness on the immediate and consider ourselves too busy to accept responsibility for being fully informed and critically active at higher levels of organizational complexity. Democracy, if it is to work as it should, is rather more demanding of time and effort than many people are prepared to meet.[30]

Shaping Society Toward Peace

This works in two ways. It means that the whole country can all too easily be rushed into a war or some other action which most of the citizens would not approve if they were fully informed and had an opportunity to discuss it and register their opinion. But it also means that there is a wide field for action open to people who want to shape society towards social justice and peace. Churches and other religious and civic groups who want to involve themselves in that work are faced with three separate tasks, first, to discern the principles or characteristics that make a society just and peaceable; second, to propose or critique policies in their particular society to realize those principles and correct existing imbalances; and third, to show their own members the role that they can play in shaping those policies. Many people in the United States understand the doctrine of separation of Church and state to imply that religious bodies should not be involved in anything like this at all. However, reflection on the meaning of the religious traditions suggests that they are not concerned with some separate realm of salvation which can be relegated to ritual observances, private life, and beyond death. Because they are concerned with ultimate human happiness, with the quality of human life, with reconciliation and the meaning and purpose of our human existence in which we are interdependent with one another, the religious groups cannot exclude from their teaching and guidance the way we relate to one another at all levels of social organization.

Discerning Principles of a Peaceable Society

Concerning the first of the three tasks, that of discerning the principles that make a good, just, and peaceable society, some religious traditions have developed much more detail than others. But one characteristic is particularly stressed by most: the obligation to look out for all, not marginating or eliminating anyone or any group, and the urgent need at all times to work with a bias towards the least privileged, the least regarded. The tendency of religious groups to do this indeed in their public utterances and positions has alienated some of their privileged members on each occasion when a major issue has been under discussion. Yet the logic is quite clear within the spirituality traditions and has only been obscured by the tendency to base religious instruction on the ritual aspects of religion.

Another characteristic that has been stressed by religious groups in their critiques and proposals for national policies is the need to consider the peoples of other nations and the impact that the policies of one's own nation may have on other peoples. In the West this has been most marked in the utterances of the Catholic Church for the obvious reason that with its worldwide extension it is in a position to be more immediately aware of the effect on the materially and strategically poorer nations of the actions of the powerful nations. But this is not a caution unique to utterances of the Catholic Church. It is matched by statements and warnings of the World Council of Churches. It is found in Buddhist utterances, in warnings of certain Islamic leaders, in the Gandhian tradition, and in many others. Yet this also is frequently rejected by members of these religious groups who want to separate national policy and their own role in it from any religious obligations which they acknowledge in their private lives. The answer to this is, of course, that relations at the international level are still relationships among human beings and subject to the same criteria of justice and fellowship as any other relationships.

Subordinating National Desires to the Desire for Peace

However, it is perhaps another criterion which raises the greatest outcry and resistance to the positions taken by religious bodies with regard to public life. It is when these groups propose the subordination of national desires to the need of peace, when they propose measures of disarmament and redeployment of resources of food production and redistribution, when they point to the availability of diplomatic means as canceling any justification for warfare, that the outcry is the greatest. Then the argument is raised that the peace teachings are impractical, idealistic, dangerous. The point is made that peace would be nice but is impossible, that if our own nation does not resort to war others will, that if we do not make war now there will be a much longer and more terrible war later, all because wars are inevitable and will happen no matter what people do to promote peace.

Critiquing Policies in Society

It is because this kind of objection and argument comes up so frequently and in the conversation of highly intelligent and sophisticated people, often of great civic responsibilities in their offices, that the religious groups must do more than make very general utterances about the value and necessity of peace and justice in society. They must attend to the second task, namely, the proposing and critiquing of policies in their societies. A significant field for action to promote peace is in the teams and studies which serve to advise religious leaders and official representatives on the technical aspects of national and international policies. This involves collaboration of economists, statisticians, lawyers and international lawyers, political theorists and those who know the machinery and working of government in detail and, according to the nature of the project, other kinds of experts and expertise.

The work of such teams and study groups enables representative and official groups to formulate positions which the membership of a religious or other body can adopt. It would be quite impossible for each individual member to work out the best policy on investment and divestment of the individual's savings and pension fund in order to move towards betterment of an oppressed population in another country, but once an expert team has formulated a policy that should help, it is possible for individuals to influence the investment of their savings. It would be impossible for all individuals to be fully informed about the diplomatic possibilities of preventing outbreak of wars or about all the issues over which wars are threatened in different parts of the world, but where competent teams have made these studies and the results are disseminated to the membership, individuals as citizens can make their voices heard.

Guiding Individuals Toward Peace Action

This points, however, to the third task that organized groups of large numbers of committed people must undertake. That is the guidance of the individuals in the memberships both by communicating the issues and the proposed action to them and by showing them the various ways in which they can participate in implementing the action. This intermediate leadership is also significant in action for the shaping of a peaceable nation and a peaceable world. Many people do not vote and do not even register to vote; they need to be encouraged and helped and informed on the issues by responsible and well-informed persons whom they know they can trust. Few people venture to lobby their legislative representatives. They need to be shown how to do this and they need to be given clear information on significant issues and on the timing of representations that may make a difference. They need to be offered motivation, to know that one telephone call or letter will make a difference because the opinions coming into legislative, executive, and party offices are counted, and to know the difference the outcome will make to the lives of real people like themselves.

There are many peace groups in existence who distribute literature, have meetings, and study their own traditional peace teachings in relation to current affairs and in relation to specific diplomatic and territorial issues that have arisen. Perhaps such groups could extend their effectiveness by playing some of the intermediate roles to engage ordinary people in the democratic channels for influencing public policy on critical issues and at critical moments.

Objectives of Peace Societies

There is another range of activities to influence social and political shaping of societies and their foreign policies. This is something that the established peace associations have frequently done, namely, a wide range of civil disobedience, protest, and demonstration activities. Though popularly regarded as the main thing that peace groups do, this type of action can never be more than preliminary and marginal. In the life of an individual conscientious objector or demonstrator, this may be the most crucial and prophetic action in which that person will ever engage, and it may take take that person to a long prison sentence, social ostracism, or death. Therefore it will be an heroic and definitive action. But in the life of a peace movement or association, this cannot be central or definitive because the objective is to shape policy and action not only to protest against unacceptable policies and actions. To work positively towards peace requires a certain acceptance by the community, competence to make proposals, patience and time to explain the proposals and persuade others of their viability, and willingness to contribute something to their implementation. Often such work involves willingness to compromise, to do the do-able now, and to strive towards the desirable in the future. Such work can be disappointingly slow in showing any results, and those who engage in it need to be peaceable in their own personality and way of going about things.

Achieving Peace Peaceably

Something that has often worked against peace movements is that their members have been committed to preventing wars among nations without realizing how important it is that in this case the means used should share the nature and quality of the end to which they were directed. By the very nature of things, the achieving of peace really has to come by peaceful means. As mentioned in an earlier chapter, the history of wars is full of declarations that the purpose of the war is to settle disputes and bring peace. This has never really worked except by the total extinction of one side, and even in such cases the residual attitudes and expectations of the survivors have created new forms of violence and oppression.

To many people the foregoing comments may seem self-contradictory because they know that changing anything in the prevailing values and policies of society involves conflict and struggle, while peaceful means seem to mean avoiding conflict. This is, in fact, a false dilemma. Conflict is not the same thing as hostility, hatred, rejection, or violence. Conflict occurs wherever there is life, even in plant and animal life. In human society there are conflicts of interest, of opinion, of points of view, of schedules, of needs, and so forth, and it is part of being human to learn to resolve conflicts without violence. Most of the time human beings do this without thinking about it very much because laws, customs, general beliefs, and understandings provide a frame of reference within which a fair solution is found and the participants are satisfied. This does not mean there was no conflict but rather that the conflict has been resolved in a satisfactory way. When cars meet at an intersection, traffic lights or stop signs resolve the conflict. When taxes raised do not meet public expenditures, the legislative body concerned may have a fierce debate before resolving the matter, but legislators on opposite sides of the debate may go out to lunch afterwards quite peaceably. This is not unknown.

To say that peace must be won peaceably does not by any means imply that it will be won without difficulty, without conflict of opinion, without vigorous debate and lobbying, without long-term efforts to win over those who prefer war or the threat of war as a solution. But it does mean that the process must be as much as possible dialogue, the sharing of vision and perspectives with the hope of building consensus. And this is also the aim and the process of democracy—not to repress opposition but to come to meet it and work towards consensus.

Conclusion:
Compassion, the Heart of Peace

The argument of this book has been drawn on the one hand from reason and common sense and on the other hand from the teachings that are more or less common to the great religions of the world. It has been argued that from reason alone we can learn that war is not the answer to the problems it is intended to solve. From faith human communities of all parts of the world and all ages of human history have drawn the hope that the peace which is so needed for human societies is also something possible of attainment. From reason alone it is possible to build up an understanding of what is meant by peace that goes beyond the absence of war to the substance of a genuinely peaceable society. From faith comes the conviction that peace is a divine gift which we can receive only upon the terms on which it is offered, terms which require an appropriate response. Sheer reason can spell out a kind of logic for peacemaking. The testimonies of the religious traditions insist that peace has a price, and it begins with a personal discipline of peacefulness. But a peaceable future also has to be nurtured in the next generation, and a peaceable nation has to be built by many levels and types of social and political action.

When all this has been said, however, and even if it had been said at much greater length and far more thoroughly, what remains is that the heart of the project of peace is compassion. When people are able to feel one another's experiences as their own, they are also unwilling to inflict hurt, to kill, to maim, to destroy. And when people are unwilling to hurt, they find other ways of settling differences, conflicts, and disputes. If enemy casualties cause us the same kind of grief as the death or maiming of our own children and spouses, we will not be willing to inflict them. If we are unwilling to go to war, we shall have much stronger motivation to develop diplomatic and arbitration channels and to use them even if they involve sacrifices of economic advantages or loss of strategic power for our own country. In fact, with a real will to maintain peace, strategic power becomes less an obsession, and with a stronger development of human bonds, material possessions are more likely to fill their appropriate place in human desires rather than being sought in useless accumulation which cannot add to happiness.

Peacemaking requires many aspects of personal discipline and nurturing. It also requires much collaboration, patient negotiation, the employment of much knowledge and of many skills. But at the heart of it all is the simple human faculty for compassion.

Notes

1. Cf. Howard P. Kainz, ed., *Philosophical Perspectives on Peace. An Anthology of Classical and Modern Sources* (London: Macmillan, 1987) chs. 1–3.

2. A very helpful overview of peace teachings in the biblical religions is that of John Ferguson, "Peace in Three Religious Traditions," *World Faiths Insight*, New Series 19 (June 1988) 37–50.

3. Cf. Mark Jürgensmeier, "Nonviolence," *Encyclopedia of Religion*, ed. Mircea Eliade (New York: Macmillan, 1987) 463–468.

4. Cf. *ibid.* p. 464 for a brief account, and Walpola Rahula, *What the Buddha Taught* (New York: Grove Press, 1974) for fuller treatment. Also: "Christ and Buddha," Selichi Yagi, *Journal of Ecumenical Studies*, vol. 27, no. 2 (Spring 1990) 306–326.

5. Cf. Geoffrey Parrinder, "Peace," *Encyclopedia of Religion*, vol. 14, 223, for a brief account of the story and its impact in later history, and *cf.* Jürgensmeier, *op. cit.*, 464–465.

6. Cf. *The Wisdom of Gandhi.* Collected and edited by Thomas Kiernan (New York: Philosophical Library, 1967).

7. John Rawls, *A Theory of Justice* (Cambridge: Harvard University Press, 1971) ch. 1.

8. For an anthology of philosophies of peace, see Kainz, *op. cit.* For some key philosophical arguments over the nature and possibility of permanent world peace, see W. B. Gallie, *Philosophers of Peace and War* (Cambridge: Cambridge University Press, 1978). For a contemporary exposition of the philosophical issues, see Gray Cox, *The Ways of Peace. A Philosophy of Peace in Action* (New York: Paulist, 1986).

9. See Roland Bainton, *Christian Attitudes toward War and Peace* (Nashville: Abingdon, 1960) and John Ferguson, *op. cit.*

10. Cf. Ferguson, *op. cit.*, 42–48, and Jürgensmeier, *op. cit.* Also: W. M. Watt, "Islam and Peace," and A. Q. Khan, "Peace in Islam," in *Peace: Chris-*

tianity and Other Religions. Studia Missionalia. vol. 38, ed. Mariasusai Dhavamony (Rome: Editrice Pontificia Universita Gregorianan, 1989).

11. On Hindu tradition relating to peace, see Jürgensmeier, *op. cit.* and Parrinder, *op. cit.* Also: M. Dhavamony, "The Hindu Way to Peace," and S. L. Raj, "Jayaprkash Narayan as a Peacemaker," in *Peace*, ed. Dhavamony.

12. Cf. Gandhi, *op. cit.*, and Robert Pickus & Robert Woito. *To End War* (New York: Harper & Row, 1970) ch. 10.

13. Jürgensmeier, *op. cit.*, 464.

14. See Walpola Rahula, *op. cit.*, ch. 8. Also: G. M. Williams, "The Boddhisattva Way of Peace," in Dhavamony, *op. cit.*

15. See Huston Smith, *The Religions of Man* (New York: Harper & Row, 1958) ch. 4.

16. *Ibid.* ch. 5, and Parrinder, *op. cit.*

17. For longer discussion of the complex relationship between democracy and peace, see Pickus & Woito, *op. cit.*, especially chs. 5 and 11. Also: Jack L. Stotts, *Shalom: The Search for a Peaceable City* (Nashville: Abingdon, 1973).

18. Cf. Pickus & Woito, *op. cit.* chs. 3, 6, and 7.

19. For a thorough discussion of issues and principles involved, see Rawls, *op. cit.*, chs. 2, 4, 5, and 6.

20. A particularly insightful critique of interests at stake is to be found in Thomas Merton, *The Non-Violent Alternative* (New York: Farrar, Straus & Giroux, 1980), a posthumous collection of essays and columns. Also: Richard McSorley, *It's a Sin to Build a Nuclear Weapon* (collected essays and columns, edited by John Dear) (Baltimore: Fortcamp, 1991).

21. The argument is set out in the *Paris Manuscripts* of 1844.

22. Herbert Marcuse, *An Essay on Liberation* (Boston: Beacon, 1969).

23. Walpola Rahula, *op. cit.*, chs. 3 and 4.

24. *Ibid.*, ch. 5.

25. For contemporary economic, social, and political implications, see ibid., ch. 8.

26. See, for example, Arthur Herzberg, *Judaism*, ch. 1.

27. Cf. bibliography given in Jürgensmeier, *op. cit.*, and comments in W. C. Smith, *The Meaning and End of Religion* (New York: New American Library, 1964) ch. 4.

28. See Parrinder, *op. cit.*

29. See Paolo Freire, *The Pedagogy of the Oppressed*.

30. The treatment of this issue is very brief here because a satisfactory exposition requires an entire volume. An existing book-length treatment is Pickus & Woito, *op. cit.* Also helpful are: Kainz, *op. cit.*, chs. 1 and 2, and Stotts, *op. cit.*, chs. III–V. Also: Francis Sweeney, ed. *The Vatican and World Peace* (Montreal: Palm Publishers, 1970) and Charles Chatfield, ed., *Peace Movements in America* (New York: Schocken, 1973).

Appendix

Selected Peace Organizations
Active in the United States

American Peace Society. 4000 Albemarle St. N.W., Suite 304, Washington, DC 20016.

Catholic Peace Fellowship. 339 LaFayette St., New York, NY 10012.

Fellowship of Reconciliation. Box 271, Nyack, NY 10960.

Fund for Peace. East 46th St., New York, NY 10017.

Institute for World Order. 777 U.N. Plaza, New York, NY 10036.

Pax Christi, U.S.A. 348 East 10th St., Erie, PA.

United Nations Association of the U.S.A. 325 East 46th St., New York, NY 10017.

(A much longer and less selective list of organizations having any sort of connection with peace activities is given in Pickus & Woito, *op. cit.*)

Bibliography

Bainton, Roland. *Christian Attitudes Toward War and Peace*. Nashville: Abingdon, 1960.

Camara, Dom Helder. *Spiral of Violence*. Denville, N.J.: Dimension Books, 1971.

Chatfield, Charles. *Peace Movements in America*. New York: Schocken, 1973.

Cox, Gray. *The Ways of Peace*. New York: Paulist, 1986.

Dahl, Arthur. *Making Peace*. Kansas City: Sheed & Ward, 1990.

Dear, John. *Disarming the Heart. Toward a Vow of Non-Violence*. New York: Paulist, 1987.

Douglass, James W. *The Non-Violent Cross. A Theology of Revolution and Peace*. New York: Macmillan, 1969.

_____. *Resistance and Contemplation*. New York: Doubleday, 1972.

Ellul, Jacques. *Violence*. New York: Seabury, 1969.

Franz, Marian C. *Questions That Refuse to Go Away*. Scottdale, Penn.: Herald Press, 1991.

Gallie, W. B. *Philosophers of Peace and War*. Cambridge: Cambridge University Press, 1978.

Gandhi, Mohandas. *The Wisdom of Gandhi*. Thomas Kiernan, ed. New York: Philosophical Library, 1969.

Gwyn, Douglas et al. *A Declaration on Peace*. Scottdale, Penn.: Herald Press, 1991.

Kainz, Howard, ed. *Philosophical Perspectives on Peace*. London: Macmillan, 1987.

Macquarrie, John. *The Concept of Peace*. New York: Harper & Row, 1973.

McSorley, Richard. *Kill for Peace?* New York: Corpus, 1970.

————. *Peace Eyes*. Washington: Center for Peace Studies, 1978.

————. *It's a Sin to Build a Nuclear Weapon*. John Dear, ed. Baltimore: Fortcamp, 1991.

Merton, Thomas. *The Non-Violent Alternative*. Gordon Zahn, ed. New York: Farrar, Straus & Giroux, 1980.

Pickus, Robert, & Woito, Robert. *To End War*. New York: Harper & Row, 1970.

Rahula, Walpola. *What the Buddha Taught*. New York: Grove Press, 1959.

Rawls, John. *A Theory of Justice*. Cambridge: Harvard University Press, 1971.

Rouner, Leroy S., ed. *Celebrating Peace*. Notre Dame, Ind.: University of Notre Dame Press, 1990.

Shannon, Thomas A. *What Are They Saying About Peace & War*. New York: Paulist, 1983.

Smith, Huston. *The Religions of Man*. New York: Harper & Row, 1958.

Smith, Wilfred Cantwell. *The Meaning and End of Religion*. New York: New American Library, 1964.

Stotts, Jack L. *Shalom: The Search for a Peaceable City*. Nashville: Abingdon Press, 1973.

Sweeney, Francis, ed. *The Vatican and World Peace*. Montreal: Palm Publishers, 1970.

True, Michael. *Justice Seekers, Peace Makers*. Mystic, Conn: Twenty-third Publications, 1985.

Vanderhaar, Gerard A. *Enemies and How to Love Them*. Mystic, Conn: Twenty-third Publications, 1985.

Zahn, Gordon. *War, Conscience & Dissent*. New York: Hawthorne Books, 1967.